John Freeman

Dictionary of the Undoing

John Freeman is the editor of *Freeman's*, a literary annual of new writing. His books include *How to Read a Novelist* and *The Tyranny of E-mail*, as well as *Tales of Two Americas*, an anthology of inequality in the United States today, and *Maps*, a collection of poems. His work has appeared in *The New Yorker*, *The Paris Review*, and *The New York Times*. The former editor of *Granta*, he is Artist-in-Residence at New York University.

Dictionary of the Undoing

Dictionary of

the Undoing

JOHN FREEMAN

MCD x FSG Originals

Farrar, Straus and Giroux

New York

MCD × FSG Originals
Farrar, Straus and Giroux
120 Broadway, New York 10271

Library of Congress Cataloging-in-Publication Data
Names: Freeman, John, 1974– author.
Title: Dictionary of the undoing / John Freeman.
Description: First edition. | New York : Farrar, Straus and Giroux, 2019
Identifiers: LCCN 2019022173 | ISBN 9780374538859 (paperback)
Subjects: Political culture—United States—History—21st century. |
    United States—Politics and government—2017–.
Classification: LCC E912 .F74 2019 | DDC 306.20973/0905—dc23
LC record available at https://lccn.loc.gov/2019022173

Designed by Richard Oriolo

Our books may be purchased in bulk for promotional, educational, or
business use. Please contact your local bookseller or the Macmillan
Corporate and Premium Sales Department at 1-800-221-7945, extension
5442, or by e-mail at MacmillanSpecialMarkets@macmillan.com.

www.fsgoriginals.com • www.fsgbooks.com
Follow us on Twitter, Facebook, and Instagram at @fsgoriginals

This book is for Sarah Burnes,

ethical compass,

and

Sean McDonald,

for adjusting the level

CONTENTS

Dictionary of the Undoing

PROLOGUE Something is very wrong with the world. The disquiet of our times feels like a pause between storms. The body braces for the next wave of thunder and rain. A new agitation lurks around the corner. It can be terrifying; it often is. Take a rest with me for a moment. Let's turn away from the spectacles we are being shown. There's time, just. Let's back away from the flickering screens. Let's plunge our hands into our pockets, or link them behind our backs, and move into the ionized air all around us. Walk, stroll, wheel. Maybe as we do, we can think about what is happening.

In many ancient tales, it is the king who is blind or blinded. Power, the tellers often warn, robs those who hold it of the ability to see. Yet we are living through a strange era. Our leaders, too, cannot seem to stop the unraveling we are witnessing. Some of them cannot see it; others simply don't care. Some of them are cheering it on, or even driving this destruction. We know this because their every move is reported upon. Never has a society possessed so many tools with which to observe the powerful in public. Our pockets vibrate with updates about their every move, each lightning strike. Then we watch ourselves watching the world burn.

This vigilance is essential. It's also exhausting. It has burned down bonds between us that are essential. Separating the watchers from the huddled. Slotting us into tribes of protest, cones of preservation—as if those two postures must be mutually exclusive. As if engagement cannot take the form of self-preservation, and full-time monitoring does not have the price—occasionally—of isolation. Of loneliness. Of pain's protective narcissism.

For one winter I bivouacked on a bluff in my apartment and set up all my tools of sight. The escalation I was watching across the globe toward autocracy had made me outraged, engaged, and then antisocial. Each night I sat up late, noting the changes in the laws of my country. I marked and collated arguments being floated that were based on lies. I tracked those fabrications as they snuck into public debate and gusted on injections of hot air and became lofty assumptions, somehow attaining the heights of accepted truth. Ideas like the notion that one group of people was better than other groups. That there was such a thing as an essential American. An essential Italian. Someone quintessentially British. Or Chinese. That anything challenging these essences was an invasion. I went online and saw other people seeing this ascension of lies, and went to protests where I met fellow travelers who felt the same. We heard our voices being heard by one another; we became part of the spectacle of sight and sound of tumult. The world burned even harder.

I don't believe the registration of our discontent was useless. Recording our dismay was and continues to be very important. But it is not enough to stop the fires we see all around us. They have now turned into infernos. Look at them now as we walk. See them in the near distance? That one scorching through public works, through health care, through education—see it turning those institutions into husks? The other one racing up hillsides on dry grass? Turning our earth into an overused fuel source? What about the one sealing off borders and turning them into stripes of ash? The ones converting our wetlands and unusable landscapes into deserts, into ruins, into development zones? The ones destroying our sense of privacy? Nothing is more naked than a house after a fire. We are living in such a house. We are standing in it looking out.

The other great price to the vigilance we've kept has been a reduction in our capacities. As if all we possess is the ability to resist. To say no, to register our disagreement. Our distrust, our disgust. Our dislike. Our contempt and our scorn. We are banding together into tribes of unshakable belief as a result of this notion, thanks in part to the technology with which we register our shouted disputes. Sometimes, under the greatest forms of control, this right is taken from us, too. Some of us are not even allowed to speak, to go online—or step into a public square—and see who shares our resistance.

What if a storm is not the correct metaphor, though? I have been speaking symbolically, so why not be specific? We are living through one of the greatest transfers of wealth in human history—of assets and money, of labor and its value—and the force that is required to continue this transfer, to make its consolidation of resources permanent, has now reached a critical level. An imbalance of power so flagrant requires violence. The beneficiaries of this situation have begun to label as fungible certain human beings. They have begun trumpeting fantasies of purity, which is what nationalism is fundamentally. Ultimately, these fantasies lead to wars, which is what humans resort to when they abandon reason or know something is unfair. Change instituted by force. It has already led to armed resistance. War is what humans turn to when their cries of pain are ultimately no longer heard.

What if the story, as I've been telling it above, is wrong, though? What if all this is merely a passing fever? What if it is more like a curse? What if it is a possession? What if our leaders are not blind and instead know precisely what they are doing, and our disquiet comes from this sneaking awareness? Doubt, our friend in times of confusion, has turned against us—inspiring paranoia. We are experiencing all this confusion. Maybe what needs to be told isn't a story at all but a kind of long psalm—a litany of mourning. Of species grief.

This book is an attempt to ask these questions. The main ones it will pose are three: What if our capacity to imagine has been so badly damaged by the information climate of our times that destruction is all we can see? What if deforming our ability to imagine the present is precisely what governments and power systems do to control us? And what if I told you we have the power to change this? I believe we do. To seize this power requires a radical change in perspective, however. To do so, we need to take one tool being vandalized before our very eyes—language—and reclaim it, and redefine what it means to be an ethical citizen in the present moment. We do not need to hunt the terms that have been weaponized into nonsense; we need to grab the words that have possibility in them and begin using them anew. Using these words expansively, carefully, and with the full extent of their meaning—even if it is first in our heads—will ultimately lead to action.

I had this revelation in the spring, a year into the long crisis that is the present moment in the United States, many years into the unfolding crises that are affecting most of the countries around the world. After my winter on the bluff, I realized I needed stronger tools if I wasn't simply going to watch and record what was happening. I packed up my long-range scopes and found, rummaging through my house, that these stronger tools lay in disrepair around me. Rusted bits of language that had fallen into disuse but still existed. Broken words that had been melted down to their simplest component parts—shorn of their complexities. These words lived in books and sometimes sprang right out there in the open from the mouths of my friends and loved ones. *All* these words were actively being mangled in public.

This book is an attempt to build a lexicon of engagement and meaning in a time and media age that has made a mockery of those forces in our lives. A time that has called out to the darkness that exists inside all of us. Each word feeds into the next word, and I hope by the book's end, at the very least one or two sparks will have been lit. So you can see how big the cave of possibility before us is, how much language—which gives us the ability to say what we mean and live within complexity—awaits our care. Our use. Our stewardship and our quest for beauty. The world in which we live calls out for this. Maybe you make your own lexicon as a result. Or maybe you simply take one word. All we need is a spark in the dark. One at a time.

Agitate

We are angry and ashamed, but mostly we are apathetic. We know the powers that be depend on it. And they have figured out how deeply that apathy extends. How far? Police and soldiers can brutally murder people before our eyes and get away with it. Politicians can lie. They can cheat. Governments can poison our water and our food. Candidates can brazenly steal elections and crow over historic victories. And the barely elected can loot our treasuries while scolding government for its ineffectiveness. Watching all this—and we are watching—has been beyond demoralizing, but what else can we do? Look away? Stop paying taxes? Who has done that? Meantime, the system of dissent and citizen input isn't working. How many bankers went to jail during the last financial crisis? How many police officers get a prison sentence for shooting an unarmed civilian? How much has been done to protect our elections from being hacked? Who pays when a pharmaceutical company wins record profits by getting tens of thousands of people addicted to painkillers? At the same time, how many people lost homes? How many working-class people are without hope? How many are in prison for assaulting an officer?

How many people of color are still in jail for smoking a joint? How many have been deported—pushed south or north or into mountains, away from where they simply want to live?

We are living through one of the greatest transfers of wealth and power in human history and there have been virtually no riots. Mass protests occur and then disperse. Citizen outrage is being controlled through violence, through the use of force in cities and towns—the brazen use of force. Law enforcement doesn't care if it's filmed. They *need* some of it to be filmed so we can see what the impunity of power looks like; otherwise the message is not sent. *They can do what they want.* Meantime, those of us who are fellow travelers to protesters and people who are paying for their beliefs with their body—or simply just for being—control ourselves. With the internet. This big machine, this panopticon, we have built one post at a time. We watch, we profess, we complain, on it goes, and thus agitation leads to apathy. And apathy leads to more digital agitation. We are not foolish for having constructed this machine. Anger and outrage make us lonely, but our inability to be alone has been used against us. Our idea that empathy is equal to action has been used against us. So we are left talking to one another and trying to maintain some semblance of value to language as it's vandalized. A body is a body, not a data point; a fact is a fact, not a subjective part of an argument. Meantime, the rate of change in this spectacle of violence we call modern life accelerates. It has reached a terminal velocity, in fact, where nothing makes sense. To simply keep up, to log the events of a day, feels like a full-time job. It makes you feel insane if you even try. And still, even if you could order and arrange all the monstrosities ongoing in our present moment, doing so would not be enough.

Knowing injustice is happening is not enough. We have to learn to turn information into action rather than apathy, because in our time apathy plagues a significant part of the population. Information is not just leading to apathy; information is *causing* it. We are burying ourselves in awareness. We know we are not putting our bodies where our beliefs are—especially those of us whose bodies have been protected our whole lives by our whiteness, by our freedom, by the fact that nothing is projected upon us. Our apathy—as in our passionately disengaged engagement—is part of the reason the struggle continues to be a struggle rather than a tipping point toward true justice. Our apathy has turned the struggle into entertainment. Our apathy has made empathy a consumable experience.

We live in agitating times. How else to describe what it feels like to be alive today? As if a rough rope has been raked over tender skin—waking it painfully. The parts of us that feel are raw now, and they're alert all the time.

For good reason. Dark forces are afoot. You feel them like a kick of a boot, a beam of light shown from a hand that holds power. A truck driving by slowly, knowing you ought to be scared. These types of gestures were once done in the dark. Or at least the half-light of shadows. Now there's a strong sense their perpetrators don't have to hide. Maybe they never did.

That feeling, that rush of adrenaline and alarm that bolts through the body in such moments, is fear. The body telling us something isn't right. An animal sense that never leaves, no matter how much we sit at a desk using our civilized skills. What civilization, though? For those of us protected by our skin color, one of the peculiar aspects of living today is we can watch the fear of others, slowly dosing ourselves with a sick kind of relief that at least it's not us. And thus the system tests us. How much are you willing to watch? How many floods before you stop driving your car? How much are you willing to sacrifice to help another in need? How long will you observe the complacency of the safe without damning them, too?

The system is testing us, and pushing us, because it's being pushed to the limit. Twenty-six people are worth half the value of the planet. Global capital and democracy depend on interconnectedness, and yet the checks and balances on these systems have been ripped off, or proven to be useless—leaving many governments wide open to corruption and manipulation. To profiteering and power grabbing. Banking regulations that were placed to prevent another collapse are all but gutted in many economies across the world. Voting rights are under attack everywhere. Environmental accords to share the burden of the disaster we are approaching have all but failed. Many governments see a distracted, apathetic populace and are grabbing more power for themselves than ever before.

Even if you don't intend to read the headlines, they're hard to ignore. Every day begins a new crisis. An item of news is channeled and elevated, then broadcast and discussed. Riffed on. We have eighty-six thousand, four hundred seconds a day, but we typically spend most of them looking at a handful of images, reading about a half-dozen stories, in thrall to a few personalities. Or maybe just one? We have all the choice in the world, yet time and again the little invisible directors in the codes that run the world draw us to a simple few. Why?

It suits the corporations and governments that hold power for us to feel this way. Agitated users of social networks click more, we know, and clicks for the media giants of the world mean huge profits. There's a reason you can't look away, too. It's not just that the spectacles our new forms of media show us are that entertaining. Some of them are grisly. Some are strange. Some are downright weird and grisly all at once. But they've been *designed for you*. Every time you use social media and the internet, data is collected on how you move in virtual space and what moves you there, and then ways are found to keep you connected. The world's most powerful artificial intelligence is being used on you, and for the price of free admission, all of us who use these tools allow it to happen.

It feels good to have a say, which is what our new media makes us feel like. To have a voice, even if it's just one among many. To have a platform, to be followed, to be liked, to be looked at and paid attention to, even if in a negative way. Yet bit by bit, as the number of social media users tops one-third of the planet, we are losing purchase on what it means to have a voice. If you speak only to those people who agree with you, what does that mean? If you are constantly being agitated by spectacles of abuse and suffering and destruction, at what point does outrage inflation run away with the essential value of language? How do you express abomination over murder and destruction when all that language has been hollowed out by small-time thieving or even just idiocy?

The governments that run the world and the technology companies that help us watch them—and one another—have an insidious convergence of strategy, perhaps unplanned but reinforcing nonetheless. Both benefit when we are frightened and enraged. Abraded. Agitated people feel more powerful because they are at least alive to something, when in fact they are more easily manipulated. Agitated voters vote—and sometimes don't, depending on what messaging they receive. Agitated consumers buy. Agitated eaters eat faster. Ever wonder why busy restaurants blast music at you? To get you out the door faster. Agitated users of social media stay connected. We are being manipulated, and so on top of the fear that we feel running through our bodies, another big one runs just behind: we are being fooled.

We are in the middle of an information war. It started well before the 2016 election, and it's not about to end, because the manipulations of social media are highly effective. They are the cheapest form of warfare ever invented. For a few million dollars the Russian government threw the United States into a paroxysm of chaos that even a catastrophic income gap couldn't manage. Nor spectacles of radicalized violence. This type of intervention is happening the world over. We are being told real news is fake and fake news is real, and the platforms that now bring us the majority of our news are washing their hands of the situation, saying that they're just platforms, not publishers.

We don't have to live like this. It's much harder to opt out of governments than it is to opt out of media, so one of the most crucial questions today is this: Are we going to grab the platforms that are still available to us—the ones that aren't being used and still would function if we could all, for a second or two or maybe longer, turn away from screens—the street, the public square, the free press (printed on paper and distributed), and the rooms of our houses of worship and schools; or are we going to continue using the ones that keep us angry and distracted, that trick us into complacency and apathy, that siphon off our data and leave us feeling lonely and afraid, dissatisfied with our lives?

We need to face this hard question if we are ever going to redefine *agitate* as an active word. When was the last time you heard it used as in to agitate for change? To agitate for justice? To agitate for fairness? To agitate for an end to corruption? This gap you're probably feeling in your memory ought to tell you that the modes of agitation have been turned against us. We can change that direction, though. We can begin by realizing that if we can't completely opt out of the system, we can at least figure out ways to build spaces within it—living, active places—that make change possible. We need to agitate against apathy.

The original agitators in our lives were people who spoke. People who took up residence in a town square or who went from house to house and looked someone in the eye and said something. Who understood the power of the eyes and ears and how much we needed to see something to believe it. For the past seven decades, since the dawn of television, we have abstracted these experiences. We've listened to and watched people on screens; we've taken our eye off the world; we've done it the easy way. We've invited them into our living rooms when we didn't even have to serve them coffee.

We can also disinvite them. In fact, we must if we are going to feel something that invites us out of the dark apathy of watching the world burn. Places all around us are calling to us. Our local chapters of unions. Our places of worship. Our parks. Our town squares. Our libraries. Our meditation centers. It is so much harder to manipulate these places. To chase optimism from them. If we are going to turn agitation on its head, we need to step away from the forms that are doing it to build dependence and instead turn toward the spaces that cannot be entirely controlled by governments and technology companies. We can take our bodies out there and agitate with them. Nothing rings like a bell like a body.

Body

We only get one. That's why it has such power. Be it large or small, freckled or tinted by the sun, black, brown, or white, your body—in a world of endlessness—is the end of you. It's where you becomes me. We formulate this translation daily inside ourselves, taking in how the world sees us or addresses us and then speaking back with that muscle in our mouth. The flex of our eyes. The tension that curls the lips without making a sound. We create ourselves in the improvisations of address—and with the many things we do with our bodies. Agitating our vocal cords to make a sound. Oppressive power wants to end that choice, of what to do with our bodies, how we speak with them. It wants to pulverize that agency. To do this, the oppressive power has to control the body, reduce it, flatten it. You are you, it says. And I will tell you what you are, what you are meant to do.

And so, in difficult times, the body can begin to seem like simply a container for pain. Rising forms of tyranny want us to think this way. That means their sadism is working. It means we have begun to do the work for them: of reducing certain populations and certain bodies to spectacle.

In our modern world there are two audiences for abuses of the body: the viewer and the person being beat, whose body is separated from them, so that its abuses entirely define them. Show this cycle of viewing often enough and the person being beaten will do the abuse for you.

Our culture has become a machine tuned to spin these images. To show us black and brown bodies being abused and women's bodies being abused, to screen pornographies of violence constantly. We consume these images and become part of them, as if there isn't a different way to inhabit our bodies. As if no one right now is boiling spaghetti. Or writing a postcard. Or downloading a TV show, or praying, or calling out in despair. Or driving slowly across a long, broad stretch of land in a car alone. Or boarding a bus, or memorizing a poem, or lifting a barbell, or holding a breast before kissing it, or laughing so hard they fall off a chair and fart, or sleeping, or weeping in grief, or weeping in anger, or shouting in anger, or putting their mouth after all these activities to a microphone one afternoon and saying, I am here.

Our job as citizens is to reprogram our culture as we hold our governments accountable to our needs. We vote and protest with our bodies. Meantime, we can make our culture an antidote to this poisonous cycle of images. We can choose to stop injecting ourselves with it, and we can find a new lifeblood. One that is based on truth—there is violence; we cannot turn away from it—but a truth that also acknowledges no body is made for harm, or better able to stand harm, than another. We can make a culture that has in its bloodstream the idea that a body is also a container for joy, and one of joy's most ferocious expressions is resistance. We all know that joy is not expressed alone. Even those unbelievers among us find it hard among the fellowship of worshippers to deny the power of joy, of bodies next to bodies expressing it together. It's why there's such tensile power in a library, all those bodies bent over books, bending toward joy in the word. You can feel it on the street some days, the best of them, walking among one another, each body a moving planet of power and joy.

As citizens, wherever we are, we have a right to the sovereignty of joy in our bodies. That means we cannot be unduly harmed, detained, beaten, spit on, maced, pinned, or choked: any institution that is doing such things has begun to lose its power. When a government begins to rely more on the instinct to coerce to stay in power, we must resist, strongly, all of us. But we must also know such governments have shown how deeply they fear the power of the body. Bodies in the street marching in joy. Bodies showing up to protect other bodies from pain. Bodies dancing, bodies adorned, bodies undressed, bodies fucking, bodies reading, bodies praying, bodies mobilized.

Each of us may get just one body, but there is a universe of complexity and intensity in every single one. Bear down hard on bodies and they will come together somewhere else, seeking joy. It wasn't the spending contest and the missiles pointed at population centers that broke the Iron Curtain; it was the beauty of blue jeans wrapped around a body. Governments, because they tend to consolidate power in the hands of a few, behave like sociopaths and sadists. They do not have the capacity, as entities, to express joy, like bodies do. It is up to us to show how that is done, and in that redefinition—we take back our bodies, and remember how much power we hold.

Citizen

A nation is a woodworker. A nation is a woodworker that often thinks it's carving a grand sculpture called *Nation*, wielding the blade of its laws. The mallet of its electioneering. The gouge of war. In fact, the sculpture a nation often makes with these chisels is the citizen.

In times of extreme nationalism, the citizen gets smaller and smaller, narrower and narrower, until only a very tiny group can recognize themselves in this miniature figurine. The nation professes its love for this creation. They agitate the airwaves with calls—We love you, O citizen; we are made by and for you—as a kind of trick, encouraging its actual living, breathing residents into worshipping an effigy: the essential citizen. Sacrifices must always be made to protect this citizen. Those sacrifices always identify the people who want to take things from that citizen. And so a population is turned into a mob or a group of tribes: those who are for the citizen and, in turn, the nation; and those who are against them.

A second, far more expansive definition of *citizen* is waiting for us in our language. We only have to claim it. Not the citizen defined by the wedges of policy, as in people recognized by a state or nation. But the citizen as defined by *who lives in a nation*. Whose bodies are there. Who occupies its territory and drinks its water and makes their homes on its land and breathes its air. Think briefly about how many fewer knives it requires to make this figurine. In fact, if you set out to make such a citizen—with all the wood in the world and all the tools—you couldn't. Instead, you would make a giant sculpture of unwieldy proportions. The armature would have to be study; it might have to be made with a material as strong as love. And there would be floor upon floor, wing upon wing. The sculpture would have to include every kind of person who actually lives in the place claimed by the nation.

Instead of there being a gap between nation and *Nation*, the two would be the same.

When the gap between nation and *Nation* no longer exists, there has either been a genocide or a radical expansion of the idea of citizenship. The reason we tremble in times of nationalism is that we know the blades of nation-carving lead us to terrible reductions. Human history is littered with them—camps, killing fields, ghettos. The logical extension of an expanded definition of *citizenship*, however, has never been achieved. The mythology of a few countries has imagined it, but few have actually lived it. What would happen if we allowed all the living bodies on our borders to be citizens? How would it feel to live in such a place? Why have all religions fought so hard to resist this? To use Christian terminology: Is it not possible that when we were asked to mimic the kingdom of heaven on earth, this is what God meant? What if the main job as citizens is to try to make this possible? What kind of nation would that be?

Decency

Of all the norms upon which civil society depends, decency is the most delicate. It exists only in practice, not in the abstract. A society, after all, is the sum of the behaviors it tolerates, and those behaviors are constantly shifting. So although it is not considered morally respectable to walk down the street shouting at people, especially those weaker than you, belittling them, and no one would tell their child to do that, that is precisely what some elected officials do. Especially in times of nationalism or power consolidation, they stand in the pulpits of modern life, these voices—not all of them elected, some self-appointed—and they tell us how the weak are not actually weak. They point fingers and claim how the seemingly weak manipulate, how they cheat, how they lie and steal. Watching such speeches from afar, or hearing them—even if you live at the greatest remove from media, you cannot escape such talk—you will feel the ground of decency shift. It needs to in order to take from the weak, as the powerful often do. On the new level, what is decent is not kindness to all, especially to those in need, but honesty in the face of a hard reality:

that we need to protect what will be taken from us by those who do not deserve it.

So many of these rhetorical gambits depend on zero-sum thinking. As if there is only so much decency to go around, and we can use it up. As if including everyone in our definition of *decency* is, in essence, indecent. No one has ever proven these assumptions about decency to be true. As with the treatment of citizens, societies tipping toward tyranny always begin shrinking their definition of *decency* by subtracting people. It is indecent to harm someone, unless they are (you can fill in the blank). It is indecent to turn your face away from suffering, unless that person is (you can fill in the blank). If you turn your ear to the wind and listen to the voices that travel on it, you will sense the proximity of brutality. There's an agitation to the way the powerful begin to speak. Repetitions, cul-de-sacs of impressions, word clusters, and nicknames become part of the syntactical tools used to chip populations out of the citizenry; *cockroaches, vermin, hordes.* It is a clawing, gnawing sound these tools make when they enact violence on the definition of *decency.* It ought to be because these words are the linguistic precursor to physical violence. It is the sound of someone trying to get inside our heads. Here's when tyranny truly takes over: when the rhetoric of zero-sum thinking becomes intimate. When either with or against your will that thinking enters your body.

We have been hearing this sound for too long. As violent as our societies are, as far as they've reduced the definitions of *citizen*, we know they could become much worse if we do not agitate back. That is one price of citizenship, true citizenship: vigilance against the corruptions of power. We will not resist a tipping into tyranny by calling for decency: it is in the interest of the very powerful to shift the definition before our very eyes. To prey upon our apathies. We will resist full-blown tyrannies, though, by practicing decency ourselves. This we have in our control. Each of us, even if we are having difficulties with mobility or live in the most remote parts of any land, encounters other people in our days—some of them are like us, some not; some of them better off than us, some not. Practice kindness to all in smaller numbers, and it slowly can be asserted as the norm. Assert an intolerance of the suffering of others, and gradually it can become the norm. Address all people with an assumption of their dignity, and it can become the norm. Behave as if everyone has an equal right to happiness, and it can become the norm. Assume the care of all human bodies, and their abuse in any form becomes an indecency our norms cannot tolerate. We have the right and the power to uphold these norms; to make them part of our definition of *decency*, we must. Asserting them will highlight the difference between our voices and those of people calling for the opposite. At which point we will not feel the need to ask them for their decency, to beg for it: we will express ours by enacting it. By voting, by living, by rejecting intolerance and protesting *indecency* from power.

Environment

Somehow we've come to think of the environment as a thing outside us. As if it were a place, or a monument built out of a rock face, or a lonely mammal swimming in the sea. When people profess among friends to caring about the environment, their voice often adopts a wistful tone. Their friends stand back to give that emotion room, and then conversation eddies back to sunnier topics. As if we are not mostly made of water or can live without clean air. As if it does not take years of determined social conditioning to teach the animal out of us. As if that animal part does not die but merely recedes into submission, watching without language as we molest and poison its home. The part of us that learns language must also develop an intense form of apathy in order to be unmoved by the sound of this animal part of us screaming. If that noise escaped from just a few more of us, it would be cacophonous. The sound would be unbearable. It is the sound of a body being tortured.

Just as the powers that be subdue the body to rule, so must they put their boot on the earth's neck to obtain and sustain that power. Would we see this abuse better if we called it a *body* rather than the *environment*? We know much of it is alive. From the trees we grow as decoration to the animals we breed. We know that the conditions much of our livestock are kept in are cruel. And yet we persist—so that we can eat meat far more often than we ought to, at prices so artificially low that a meal is no longer anything close to a celebration or a ritual.

We are beyond the point of this being a mere character flaw. Our needs as humans have for so long superseded the needs of any other species on earth that we are using up the resource that has sustained us all, and it is fighting back. Heating up, breeding superviruses, throwing up catastrophic weather events. Meantime, most of the species that have ever lived are now dead. We have murdered them for tidier cup holders, plastic straws, the ability to drive a two-ton vehicle by ourselves a distance we could walk so we can drink a beverage harvested from beans grown six thousand miles away out of a cup that will take three lifetimes to deteriorate. Pause to appreciate the astonishing gluttony of this act and its costs. The part of us that is animal is still screaming, but we push it down, we get back in our vehicle the size of the animals that once lived freely on the savannas, and we drive another mile back to a temperature-controlled home with endless water and light.

We, the small but powerful few who live amid these conditions, have lost the ability to conceptualize the indecency of it. So we must now redefine what the environment is to us. As rational thinkers, we know inequality to be created by a consolidation of power and resources. You do not need to take an economics class to understand that unchecked inequalities inevitably reach a critical mass and lead to tyranny. In the world of humans, we have reached this critical mass. Just twenty-six people are worth the collective labor of more than three billion people. Think of all the waking and lifting and sweating and weeping and breaking and healing and waking again that simple statistic means. Bottle the sound of all that work. Hear its keening. Now think of the earth. Humans are just one of its approximately 8.7 million species. Yet we consume all its biocapacity and then some. In ten years, we will need a second planet to support ourselves.

Our relationship to the environment is an indecency. And yet we have made a silent pact with the powers that be that makes this condition far worse: it says, I will turn my face from this gluttony in my name, and you can continue to enrich yourselves beyond all imagining. Enormous fortunes are not made from thin air. They are produced by seizing the resources and labor of many and putting them in the hands of the very, very few. If we are ever to become ethical citizens in the places where we live, we need to recognize this cycle and its costs. To recognize that inequality among humans is always connected to inequality among the earth's species, to whom we are like those twenty-six mega-billionaires. We must learn to listen to the animal agitating for change inside us, and those all around us, and reengineer our lives away from the activities that we know depend on torture—of animals, of the land, of the sea, of the air. We know what to cut back on. We know where we can scrimp and save. Our bodies have been telling us in all the languages but the ones we speak.

Fair

The word *fair* is like a mirror we think is a window—instead of looking through it at the world and all its phenomena, we peer back at ourselves. What do we see? It depends on where we look. Is it fair that at this moment a polar bear is drowning in a rising sea? Is it fair that a fish on its way to spawn will become that bear's meal? Is it fair some people live longer than others? Is it fair the rich are taxed at higher rates? Is it fair they can afford accountants who ensure the rich never pay such rates? Is it fair that I am typing this from a warm home while someone else is in a prison cell? Is it fair my skin color allows me second and third chances while others barely have one? Would it be fair to make a world that rights this balance? How much should be taken from me to do it?

Every time we try to polish fairness to lucidity, it reasserts its relational optic. Fairness is the glass that never allows you to look at another without seeing yourself. In this way it is an essential value in any society, which by definition functions by giving people a sense of order so they can live together. So they can see one another. A society edging toward tyranny has an enormous gap between what people consider to be fair and how the society operates. It often also sees in only one direction: toward the ruling class, the powerful, or just one man. Any suffering outside this group isn't seen. Everyone knows this is unfair, and this kind of unfairness, rampant and unchecked, creates apathy in citizens. In this way, dictators and titans sometimes control the people below them through their agitating demonstrations of unfairness. The brazenness of this narcissism is a numbing narcotic. Think of how much time our society spends gazing at the rich and the powerful. Our fabled leaders. In this way they become gods, not in that they are eternal but that they are living outside the rules of mere mortals. And of fairness.

It is possible to claw back from the precipices of tyranny if fairness does more than exist as a concept to be publicly flaunted. For a society to function fairly, it cannot always be up to those on the losing side of change to affect change. In fact, it is better if change comes from a joint effort between the so-called beneficiaries and the losers of political change. Both sides looking through the window and seeing themselves in the glance of their society. Otherwise, history becomes nothing but a power struggle—the powerful taking from the weak until the ruling class loses enough power to be taken from themselves.

We are animals at heart, but the difference between

us and them is the sophistication of our consciousness. It's not just that I can think, I am me; like most humans, I also developed around age four or five a theory of mind, which means I can extrapolate from I am me to therefore, you are you. In this cognitive development, human beings become capable of recognizing the difference between fair and unfair. As children, we all recognize unfairness because we feel the sting of not getting what feels like our share. Our equal slice of pie. Our equally long hug. Our equally long ride on a bicycle. Our chance at happiness. Children become nicer when they learn theory of mind and unfairness becomes three-dimensional, because they can inhabit the unfairness of others and do things to alleviate it, like sharing.

There is an immense fork in the road for most humans at this point, though. Some of them are taught that fairness is the norm, and anything other than that should not be tolerated. Others are taught that fairness ought to be the norm; yet it is not, so they must learn to cope. The gap between these versions of reality is as wide as the gap between the words *just* and *equitable*, the two concepts upon which fairness stands. Justice depends on how a society prosecutes injustice with the laws it writes. All children learn quickly that some of those laws are unfair. In the meantime, equity is a far easier notion to square—it is not so necessary to adjudicate. All you have to do is ask, Is what you have the same size as and scale of what I have? Even though such measurements can be warped by subjective perception, they can be measured. Have you lived a day recently without coming across some measure, some form, of inequality?

We know that inequality feels miserable, that riches enjoyed in the presence of suffering are spoils, and that suffering when great wealth is being piled up all around us feels even more like misery. If we are ever to change such things, we need help remaking the word *fair*. We cannot do it alone. Glass is made by heating sand to a temperature none of us can achieve in our ovens, and then letting it cool. When nuclear scientists tested the first atomic bomb in the deserts of New Mexico, the explosion was so powerful it turned the sand around it to glass. So it sometimes must be with societies and fairness. They settle and settle like silt into patterns of unfairness, and then a superheated rupture needs to occur for them to create fairness again. Sometimes that heat is made by protest; sometimes it is made by trauma. In the best of times, it is made by debate, by the friction of concepts rubbing up against one another in open space, creating an intense fire. By a positive agitation. At the end of which things cool and there's a new kind of fairness. Even then it will not be an entirely transparent pane. Like glass is to a mirror, it will be more like a frozen liquid resting up against something silver, and noble. A frozen snapshot of what our society made into law resting up against the eternal inner sense of equity—the one we recognize in the way we know when the moon is out before looking up.

F

Giving All of us know whether we give enough. There's no chart. It travels inside each of us, this secret knowledge. One might say it's like an invisible level. Have we given or have we looked away? We do not need to have handed over money. It could be something small, like a sweet, or something big, like our labor. Have we carried something for another? Have we donated our expertise? It sounds strange, but at our lowest, we can be lifted out of the depths by our own giving hands. Giving is apathy's kryptonite: apathy doesn't stand a chance once we start to give. Why? So many of us have more than we need. All of us know this situation, this imbalance of the world, is an indecency. It's almost as if evolutionary biology is working with us to bring out our best selves. To reshape an environment in which to be human is to give. Giving brings a body joy we know. It agitates toward pleasure. It is becoming a psychiatric fact that giving feels good on a cellular level. You give and your body rewards you in the same way it pats you on the back when you work hard, when you sleep, when you exercise: your body floods with the chemicals of happiness.

Our societies are meant to be structures of giving.

You could almost make it part of the definition of *citizenship*. What are citizens? They give. Everyone eventually needs, even all the way to kings. Spreading that need is how governments function. Yet we are nearing the end of a radical experiment in eradicating the giving impulse in government. Policy makers are stripping away what can be given; and when that can't be removed, they are pulling back on the hands that can be extended; and when those can't be stopped, they are labeling the hands that receive as illegal or undeserving; and when those receiving hands can't be reduced or criminalized or shamed, they are eliminating whole departments so that if giving is to continue, it needs to become an underground economy. A black market in giving. And this has happened. Look around your community and you will notice organizations have sprung up to do what the government once did or promised to; almost all these activities involve giving. Giving someone a home; giving someone health care; giving someone counseling; giving someone food; giving someone a chance to finish school. It's how we are decent, building such groups and communities. It is how we redefine fairness outside the circles that malign the concept. This black-market economy in generosity is part of the ways bodies, when borne down upon, reassemble in schools of joy, which is to say resistance.

What is a government that doesn't give? It is a license to steal. Governments are supposed to consolidate power so they can redistribute resources fairly based upon their laws, and they take from all citizens and non-citizens in order to do that. A little bit of all our power, a little bit more of all our money. If governments have been seized by people who stop giving, or thwart this essential activity, that doesn't mean that they have stopped taking from citizens, or that they have begun dispersing power to all. A government that has stopped giving very often hasn't stopped giving at all. It has begun to give power only to the few, and if it's hard to see whom power is given to, chances are your government is giving to itself, or to the very rich. This is corruption.

Once this rot becomes visible, it usually means the entire foundation of a civic society has begun to sink. To collapse. It means it is time to start over, from the very foundation up. This is some of the hardest giving we, as citizens, may have to do. When we feel used up, abused, hard done and overlooked by the very governments that were supposed to serve us, we have one final act of giving to do—aside from building civic structures outside those governments so we can still function as a society. We need to give our hearts and minds to reenvisioning how our governments can work. We need to fight corruption by calling it out, by using the structures of society to prosecute it. To prosecute *those* receiving hands. Otherwise we will wind up in a world in which giving actually goes one way, toward the powerful. And that is not a world any more than a dark star used to be a sun.

Hope

Hope is less an emotion than a field, a magnetism. Put bodies near each other and hope happens. Very few musical concerts unfold in a wash of disconnected cynicism. Or sporting events. Or religious services. Anywhere people gather in anticipation or ritualization of a possible outcome. Shared anticipation feels like a charge. Indeed, when people gather to worship, they often leave more hopeful, less because of the scripture than because of the feeling of being around one another. Bodies tilting away from darkness—this is what hope really is, and it's so present in some places you can feel it crackle like electricity, a power that isn't worth anything until it's agitating an action. Here's why hope is necessary for any society: you can't store it, hoard it, brag about it, or turn it entirely into a weapon. Hope operates as a positive charge between people, and then it wants to move. Like all power, it wants to be transferred. One of the most effective ways to do this is to turn it into words.

In times of tyranny, governments bear down upon and try to break words so that we cannot take the power that emerges in the field of hope and transfer it to one another. They break away at the meaning of words, one sound bite at a time, like jackhammers crumbling concrete. Like someone shaving down the copper of a conducting wire. And then once the words are pulverized and nearly dust, once they are so dulled you can barely hear meaning traveling through them, the powers that be dare us to use them again. Can you call something true when so many untrue things have been asserted from a position of power? How can you claim something is, say, fair, when patently fair things have been called unfair? How can you use the word *love* when it has been used to describe political actions that are hateful? This violence against language ultimately has a cost on our private lives. Try to use language in times of crisis and it can seem like words turn to ash in our kitchens. It's like someone speaking to you through a very faint telephone line. Sometimes you can use only your body to say what you mean.

Governments do not do this violence to language because they are linguists. They do it because language is designed socially, between us, just as hope emerges in a collection of bodies. If you can attack language, you can begin to uncouple the ability for people to mean anything to one another, and in so doing, shut down the chance for hope to happen. Language, of course, is not just hope's power lines, dipping and rising between uprights from town to town; language powers the entire reality show, too. Without language the screen goes blank, and we very quickly become gestures and impulses, the needs of our bodies. We become our worst fears. Fear doesn't require language. It works on images, on smells, on drumbeats. You know someone wants you to be afraid when they try to use language like a flickering image.

Part of being a citizen today is being vigilant to abuses of language happening before our eyes and ears—noting them, sharing this information, and resisting these molestations so we can maintain a climate in which hope can still be transferred. So change remains possible. To do this we need language to create and maintain a reality that moves from people up, not from government down. Words and their meanings are very difficult to preserve in isolation. No monk is sitting in a mountain fastness preserving the precious conveyance device that is language. But people are bearing witness. Prison diaries and captivity narratives are often far more than records of a condition survived. They are a record of the person writing to themselves, making two out of one by picking up the pen. In that division—of the eye from the I—a person bearing witness to their own condition does two things: they create a collective in which language can exist, and they create a field of hope. Often in conditions that seem the most impossible for hope.

For hope to be reignited on a societal level, though, there needs to be some kind of gathering—at least two people at first, using words between them with agreed-upon meanings—for the power lines of language to begin humming again. We may start it by ourselves, writing to ourselves, or reading literature or liturgy in which language is used beautifully: this is how books create hope, even when they are not themselves beacons of optimism. The reader responds to the writer's call to be an imagined other. But we create momentum when an imagined two becomes an actual two through the use of language between us. One letter at a time, one message at a time, we can keep the power of language alive by using it truthfully, as if it matters. Saying things that matter. Saying, I saw this; I remember how this happened. And, I hear you or I see you or I care for you. In those exchanges, you will almost catch the moment the field of hope springs back to life.

In times of crisis, the internet can be a useful tool for keeping hope alive, because it can move power when bodies cannot move. It can move words when words are illegal. Indeed, it can transfer hope rapidly, at the speed of electricity, if we are not using it merely to distract ourselves from our desperation. One of the most important collectives the internet can build is between those without hope and those with it. The nimbleness of hope in digital form in a repressive world is devastating to dictatorships and autocracies. This is why the internet is strictly controlled in all the world's repressive societies.

In societies where the body and speech are not restricted, though, the internet can sharpen the damage of tyranny; because the internet is not a collection of bodies, its ethics can carom away from decency. People say things to or about one another that they would never utter in person—if there was a face on the other side, listening. We are angry and we are afraid and we are ashamed of the wreck we have made of the world, and in these conditions, people yearn for someone to blame. It is far easier and more enjoyable to flame and blame than to build a collective out of a larger sense of shared existence. In these moments of weakness, tyrannies win because *we are breaking the bonds out of which hope develops.*

The immediate remedy for these demonstrations of unkindness is for those in societies in which speech and movement remain free to step away from virtual interactions and get into the street. To stand and browse and pray and eat and walk and be among one another. Even in repressive societies, there are almost always more people than guards, than watchers, than foot soldiers. In free societies, that is especially so. That remedy instantly creates momentum when we head into the street to protest. A protest, after all, is an attempt to turn a group of bodies into a sentence, saying, *We want more*. In that sense, protests may begin in anger, but they often bend toward hope. This conductive quality is why governments need to control protests. Why they have become experts at crowd control, at subterfuge, at apathy creation. At provocation. At turning agitation against us. Governments know even more than their citizens that hope is the thunderstorm before the rain of change. And even schoolchildren know life cannot be sustained without water.

We hear a lot about ourselves on the internet—our meals, artfully presented; our last night on the town, glamorously recorded; our daily thoughts, attentively dictated. The internet is all about us. It is a surging, frothing current of first-person-ness. Our reactions to news. Our pets and their funny habits, our faces adorned with inspiring quotes. Our faces after a breakup or before a new date. Our bodies after a diet or before a diet, or in between, just needing praise. We share lots of these snippets of our lives; way too many of them, in fact, especially the good news and the good photographs. Is it any wonder that some of the most popular technology the world has ever made—from the iPod to iPhone (even if the *i* in their names was meant to stand for *internet*)—begins with the letter *I*? That "I" has long since meant, in everyday use, "me."

Long before it normalized a reality-TV sociopathic present, social media normalized narcissism. On social media, it is considered normal to talk about yourself a lot of the time. To talk about yourself in the third person. To take pictures of yourself endlessly—as if you were a celebrity and your own paparazzi at the same time. It is natural, even if you are a "friend" and not a friend of a person displaying such obvious need, to like the photo. Clearly they are asking for regard. It's easy to give. But since social media is driven by algorithms, it sees that like and sends us more photos akin to it: photos of people in states of fabulous repair, making us—sitting wherever we are, in sweats, or less—think that perhaps we should smarten up.

Not long ago, before the invention of social media, it was common in some Western countries for people to spend more time with their computers than with their spouses. Now that is the case for people with their mobile phones, and what was once a communication device has become a kind of mirror. If your phone has social media downloaded onto it, and chances are that it does, you can parcel out moments of boredom to see how many likes your latest post received, how many reactions your latest shared photograph is getting, how many times people you have never met have forwarded your latest pithy reaction to someone else's pithy reaction to a commented-upon piece of news. The mirror is always there and it feeds us. Every time we look into it, we get a reward—a comment, a like, a reaction—and a tiny blip of dopamine pulses through our system. It is the same feedback loop a slot machine works on. Technology has always been a prosthetic, but think of the ways it is now driven by a powerful cognitive-conditioning circuit: each loop teaches us to need more constant multichannel feedback and regard.

These tools are changing us, and it's worth asking, Do we want to keep going down this road? and also, Is the road big enough? Everywhere one meanders on social media or the internet, there's a phalanx of I's already there, saying what happened, digesting (and often criticizing) who was there, and reporting what they thought of it, causing one of the most common modern sensations of a heavily digital existence to be FOMO—fear of missing out. Given the tools and broadcast capabilities of journalists, a significant portion of heavy users of the internet are weaponizing their social lives and applying the tones of digital social life—glibness and a crystallized cult of personality worship born out of celebrity culture—to politics and world events.

Is it any wonder we're crippled by apathy? Apathy is the natural response to this tidal wave of agitating self-regard. Apathy is also hard to turn off once it's on, and it is not a subtle directional defense. It's difficult to draw up one's shields in one corner and be wide open in another—especially when the rise of social media has eroded the very notion that we can all even fit on the same beach. We're all so in love with the idea that we control our own wave machine that we don't realize day by day that this new culture of narcissism is drawing tyranny closer and closer. Even as our dependence upon it—the power it requires, the metals and minerals our devices need—poisons our environment.

We need to step away from time to time. The internet is not the world; it is a dream that distracts us from the world itself. While the internet came into being, we slept through one burst of development after another. When we blinked our eyes and finally looked up, many of us wondered where our local bookstores had gone, our pubs, our post offices, our newspapers, our hardware stores, our coffee shops, our florists; anything requiring the word *our* has ironically been put under threat by the greatest communication device ever created as it tipped toward the intense and endless empowerment of the word *I*.

Why shop locally when you can shop for a bargain globally? Why go to a park when you can stay in your backyard? Why overnight in a friend's guest room when you can rent a home from a stranger who is out of town? Why ride public transport when you can hitch a ride with an out-of-work actor? Why read the newspaper when you can follow the newsfeed on a social media hub that has carefully selected and curated information to show you exactly what you want from the world?

The word often used to describe this interaction between our entitled digital self and the world is *freedom*.

Of course we are free to shop wherever we please, and who wouldn't patronize a global retail giant over a local store if everything there costs half as much? The so-called invisible hand of the market is in fact encouraging us, as consumers, to make that choice. It says, you people here—on the internet—have won the competition for business, so you are free to reward companies as you see fit. Part of the modern twenty-first-century you—the adorned, well-regarded you—is that you are the chief. You are the decider. Thousands of messages sent to us on the internet every day are telling us just that, begging that, saying that it is all about you. Make the choice.

In our modern life, though, we all too often confuse freedom with liberty: the ability to act without restraint with the ability to act without oppressive restrictions. They are not the same—reasonable limits to our behavior is the definition of *civil society*. And if decency, fairness, and a tiny bit of generosity do not enter the picture, we begin to emulate in miniature fashion the tyrannies we would be so wise to resist. Thrusting ourselves forward as individuals when in fact we would be much more powerful if we stepped forward as a we.

It is not hard to rebuild that pronoun. Stepping away from the internet, if only for a short time, helps. Putting away the telephone while one does can help, too. Not every moment has to be recorded to be valuable; what can be of value is the experience itself. When that experience is based upon an interaction with another human being, thinking twice before turning it into something fungible is a form of resistance. *We* is created through privacy as well as visibility. Through asserting the right to speak and form groups and have interactions that are not commodified. We know when we begin polishing an experience for consumption. The kind of *we* that our societies need to build ought not to be the kind that is for sale. It is a complicated *we*, a fractious *we*, a thoughtful *we*, a slow *we*, a *we* that moves at the speed of conversation, not product cycles. A *we* that is durable and decent, a *we* that looks outward and tries to invite people in rather than remind those who aren't here that they have missed out.

The internet began as a defense tool; it was a fail-safe network for the U.S. president and American nuclear scientists to use to communicate in the event of a catastrophic nuclear attack. How else would people talk if all the phone lines were down? How would a president get accurate information about cities if he couldn't hear from people in them? Once it became clear this was not as urgent a threat as American scientists had feared, they began to use that fledgling network to share computing power from the few supercomputing systems scattered around the world. The computers were so big and so expensive, only a few institutions could have them.

A few years into this study in sharing, a group re-searched the early internet to see how it was being used. Their findings were shocking. Here were these comput-ers as big as houses, with long wait times to perform key data-crunching operations. Very few scientists were dialing into them remotely, though. Instead, it appeared they were using this powerful, defense-born tool to do one thing and one thing only: to chat and send messages to one another. Perhaps that is where we must return if we are ever going to rebuild our capacity to even say the word *we*. Step back and remember what a miracle it is that we can do so in the first place.

Justice

I searched for the word *justice* on the internet today, and the first thing to emerge was a line of clothing for tweens. Soon thereafter came Justice, an alt-synth band whose style is described as nu-disco. Farther down, there's a definition: the maintenance or administration of what is just or, essentially, fair. It's hard to think of a better metaphor for the state of many societies today than this order of justice. Though built and maintained by fairness, or at least a hope that it can occur, our societies are poised at a crossroads. Many of our justice departments are being hollowed out from within: either co-opted by radical executives or slowly eroded by a corrosive acid wash of money. There is, too, the possibility that the arc of justice, as it has been described, is no more than a burning moat—an unpassable ring protecting the powerful from the rest of the world. How to believe justice is an arc when all we're seeing are embers? The casual destruction of bodies by the arm of justice gives credence to the belief that maybe the system of justice was in fact built to maintain injustice. Not to prosecute or correct it. How many wealthy criminals get slaps on the wrist while others without resources go to prison? It's possible that when you open the book of our cultures, you won't read a story of justice, of citizens agitating to define the terms of their lives, but rather a tale about pain.

We have good reason to be possessed by these concerns. The internet, for all its distractions, has placed us in a new kind of simultaneous time. The digital world does not have time zones or dark hours. This means that the sparks shooting off that burning river between us and the promised land of justice are landing constantly. It can feel like a Catherine wheel. Young men shot for simply standing together on a street. Girls assaulted on buses because they were alone. Elderly people preyed upon by snake-oil salesmen pushing bad financial instruments. Public parks being cracked open like rare ostrich eggs to be consumed by a precious few, as if the environment were an untapped resource. On and on. Citrus-scented executives retiring from public life after committing larceny. The bloodlust of killers seeking its relief in conflicts around the globe. We see it all in real time.

The apathy these chimneys of injustice can produce is strong. It can make you never want to wake up some days. It can give you the sense that the law is a weapon most people learn to use to hurt others. History, however, tells us a different story. For every lawyer lining their pockets with the gains of legal extortion, dozens and dozens of others live with threadbare pockets so that they can help the most vulnerable. We must remember that power is a neutral value. In our current climate, we see spectacle upon spectacle of its abuse—many of them shown to us in order to control us. Part of that kind of power is its ability to project itself. Meantime, power can also be expressed in the ability to give, to love, to volunteer one's services, to listen, to advocate on behalf of others, and to fight injustice. These are the kinds of power that push up from the people, the ones that can move a justice system. Power is not limited to overwhelming force; power can be the slow, sustained effort to push a terrible boulder up a very long hill until suddenly there is no more slope. Power can mean the ability to define the struggle as meaningful.

To live in modern culture—which sees itself, as it's simultaneously being itself—one needs what the poet John Keats called "negative capability." The ability to hold two contradictory ideas in one's head without searching after fact or reason. We are rank, and yet we have beauty. We can produce kindness, and yet our systems of living can also become factories of pain. We are selfish, but most of us cannot tolerate a life without one another. We are racist, though we can transcend these instincts or at least protect against them with the law. There are people who learn the law so they can advocate on behalf of orphaned migrant children, whom many of our societies are trying to deport. There are also those who learn the law to rise into or maintain their status in a class that has its boot on the throats of those very children.

How to live with this contradiction? We need to be able to believe our societies can be just even as they produce swathes of injustice. To create enough space within justice as a concept for this contradiction is not to tolerate the abuse of justice but a way toward seeing how dependent justice is on our input. Justice does not run of its own accord until we need it. Justice is a system maintained by its citizens, even when governments are trying to use it to redefine what a citizen may be. Here's why we need to be involved. Justice depends upon opposing positions. There needs to be a case—something versus something else. Someone versus someone else. Someone versus their very own state. We cannot walk away from what we imperfectly made, wherever we live: our responsibility as citizens is in part to help balance it. To put our fingers, our bodies, our wallets, on the scale when we see it tipping away from the power of the people and toward the power of the few.

The law is a text, and in most cases, it has the ability to be continuously written, refined, and reshaped so that it can continue to adjudicate the disputes of changing societies. We can be part of this editing process; we must be part of it unless we want to watch laws get written or passed that harm our societies. One of the great and shameful elements of modern politics is its attempt to write citizens out of the legislative process, from purging people from voter rolls for felonies, to gerrymandering voting districts, to the expansion of corporate rights so that many companies now have more freedoms than humans do, to the way legislation gets made and debated with so much input from lobbies and special interests. Many pieces of legislation are hundreds of pages long, written quickly and in the dark, voted on in the sour hours of the night, and padded with addenda not one representative could ever utter over breakfast. This is the circadian rhythm of shamelessness. They hope we are too busy, too distracted, too apathetic, and too tired to protest. They know we are.

Here's one thing that should always give us hope, though. There are many, many more of us than there are of them. If we live in democracies, they need us for our votes; wherever we live, they need us for our tax revenue. In the realm of political action, *I* becomes *we* very rapidly. Justice may not be blind, it may give too much respect to the size of one's wallet, but it does respect momentum. As citizens, we can enforce justice ourselves outside the justice system: by gathering and mobilizing and making ourselves into groups that, because of our size, ironically reinforce the value of the small. Of one. Therein lies the contradiction that powers our justice systems: it is only by acknowledging our vulnerability to justice that we can get it to work on our behalf.

Killing

Many of us have benefited from killing. The food we eat often began at the end of another being's life. It's the same for the clothes we wear, especially if they're leather. The products we smooth on our faces have been tested on small, unseen furry creatures. So has the medication that keeps us alive, or well, or just happy. The bottle caps. The eraser tips. Anything that touches our skin, really. But it's not just animals. The streets, if they are empty and safe at night, have often been cleared by brutality enacted upon human bodies. Many cellular phones we use were assembled in workshops where conditions are so severe that children working in them have committed suicide. This is killing. Economic murder is often involved when someone is making a killing; we just don't see it. Or the connection between the act and us buying or using a product has been deliberately uncoupled by broadcast mythologies—advertising, really. If we live in the West, the price of just about every good and service has been pressed down by killing. Whether it is the gasoline we put in our cars or the diamonds some of us wear on our hands. If we got a shock every time we touched an object touched by killing, we would be electrified constantly. Like Ferris wheels, we circle our days illuminated by the power of other invisible bodies in pain.

Being a global citizen today means doing one's research about the things that touch us. We live in a vast and complex political economy powered by an endless—some would say rabid—search for low-cost labor. In many countries, workers used to be organized. Unions protected teachers and machinists and meat packers against the tyrannies of ownership and, in turn, the fluctuations of markets. These were not perfect entities, unions—they could be brutal, corrupt, vainglorious, and greedy as well. But they did protect workers to a large extent. They agitated against the powers that be to create a buffer between labor and its globalized abstraction into currency markets, commodities bazaars, mutual funds. They essentially said that labor is a human body.

That is no longer the case. In the past forty years, we watched as self-proclaimed gentle but strong leaders broke these unions, one after another. Almost all these corporations repaid presidents and prime ministers for doing this wet work for them by taking their manufacturing overseas to countries whose poverty was beyond imagining, to nations that were happy to keep subhuman wages, dangerous work conditions, and no-loyalty contracts legal. Or at least to look the other way. This, we have been told for a long time, is how the world will become more equal. By working some countries' populations to death for the benefit of the few. For giving the next generation a chance at leisure.

The chances are, if you own securities, you, too, have benefited from this system. No company is going to advertise itself to you by showing you glossy brochures of its inhumane factory conditions. Very few billionaires will brag about how cheap they are to our faces. The richest individual in the world—whose net worth is greater than two-thirds of the world's nations—is refusing to pay livable wages in some of the countries where his company does business. He is being sued in many of these places. He is also using the global tax system within an inch of its life to avoid paying taxes. Is this killing people? Yes, it is. How many people struggling on an unlivable wage develop heart disease? How many people turn to drink? How many people fall asleep at the wheel? How many of them pull the trigger of a gun to make the pressure stop?

We live in a strange society when it comes to the visibility of violence. Our music and movies are full of stylized killing. Balletic performances of sociopathic revenge. We need these waltzes of small-armed explosions to expiate the rage that living in a society of aerated killing builds up in us. Who am I, you might think, to change a global supply chain? Who am I to stop a man on a quest to be the world's first trillionaire? How many corpses does one have to see "over there" on screens before the body experiences a kind of toxic shock? A sudden and terrible sense that when seen globally, fairness and order are lethal fictions, because they enable dreams those in the powerful countries need to sustain in order to live with themselves? Note that the world's only remaining superpower also possesses the most well-articulated myth of exceptional moral value in the world. Let us ask ourselves why a country built on the back of stolen labor—and, in essence, torture and killing—needs such a thing?

There is killing, there has been killing, and there always will be killing so long as we live in a world that cedes a vast majority of the right to violence to our states and to our corporations. We can alleviate this killing, though, and reduce it to a bare minimum if we refuse to participate in it. If we stop buying products built upon the torture of animals, if we stop shopping at online bazaars that do not pay a livable wage, if we stop ordering coffee at chains that tolerate the racial discrimination of their customers, if we stop patronizing businesses that do not behave decently. We live in a world in which corporations, wherever they are, enjoy the same rights as human beings. They are protected by the power of free speech, rights to privacy, and, very nearly, to the unspoken right to happiness. They are abstract human beings, corporations, and just as we keep our distance from sociopaths, so should we with companies acting like them.

Being a global citizen today means doing one's research about the things that touch us. What does this mean? It involves those of us with more leisure time figuring out how that leisure and convenience is being purchased and made. There's always a cost. Is it because rain forests in Brazil are being leveled? Is it because a cadre of career soldiers is being sent into one country after another to destabilize governments so that the world's richest stores of natural gas and oil are in the hands of a bribable few? These things are easy to find out. The internet might be a distraction tool, but it can also be used just as easily as the fastest, vastest, most connected library ever built. The shelving carts move so swiftly in it, we cannot even see them.

Those of us in the developed world have a responsibility to do this research because our governments and corporations are killing in our names. We know they are, because every time they are caught doing it, they claim to be protecting our ways of life; they talk about their dedication to their consumers. They rarely say *shareholder* publicly, corporations, because that would raise the questions: How many of us are shareholders? And why do the rights of shareholders supersede the rights of other human beings? Once again, here is a system of inequality that depends on our apathy, our busyness, our own legs being so tired from treading water we cannot extend a hand. Give a little of our time.

We need to remember, though, this killing is being done in our names. We are named in those moments because both nations and corporations believe we are powerless to contradict them. They have largely been right. How do we turn this around? We know we must. Most of us see ourselves as decent, and we wear that decency in the sounds we make, the ways we walk, and how we project ourselves.

What if we spent a bit more time on how we painted hope upon ourselves? What if our costumes acknowledged a bit more that a great many of us have been the beneficiaries of killing? What if we had the capacity to imagine an environment in which killing was intolerable and made more instantly visible? What if justice were swifter than the assumptions it had to outpace? All this depends on us. If you have ever watched power crumble, you know it happens very suddenly. One day a wall is up, and the next it is coming down. One day a powerful man is untouchable; the next he is finally being called to account for raping women he was supposed to employ. One day a company's stock value is worth billions; the next it is in bankruptcy because it lost the trust of the market. There are many, many more of us than there are of them. If we begin to say in small groups, and then bigger ones, that the killing has to stop, we'll be surprised how far we get, and what it feels like not to be standing up to our ankles in the blood of others.

Love

Love is the opposite of killing. It presses its lips to the breathless body and blows. It extends a hand, an arm, a stabilizing elbow to an elder. Love gives up its seat, hands over change, and steps aside as children get off the bus. Love only gives, because giving is love. In all these ways and others, love is like water. It finds ways quietly, persistently, to move through the world. Making life possible. And just as any environment in which we live has been shaped by water, we are shaped by love—and those of us who aren't are formed by its lack. In this regard, the most radical, hopeful act one can perform as a citizen is to love deeply, freely, and articulately. Perhaps the receiver's cup will overflow and they, too, will have no choice but to give. This is how a decent society is built, outside its laws and its continual quest for justice. All of us have reservoirs of love we do not give. We need to set them free.

A society's emotional health cannot be regulated by the few strategically placed givers among us. Queen ants of love. Handing and delivering, connecting. Supergivers. A love ungiven is like a well that has been sealed shut. It quenches no thirst, and it allows no crops to grow. The love ungiven gradually turns brackish and viscous, and then into something unlike love, such as regret or bitterness. An agitation running on a loop. Some people can seem incapable of receiving love; chances are they grew up on the outside of such a well, dying of thirst. The decent thing to do is to love them anyway; for even if time is limited, we are not given a limited amount of love. Giving love creates more love, and more energy to give it. The notion that love is ours to spend, or that it is a transaction, shows how deeply we've internalized the system of capitalism under which we live. Not every resource we have is fungible; love sometimes is only that: love.

And we do not have to speak it for it to be heard: some days even a gesture will do. We can press down into our lives with love and etch them with care. How we speak to others; how we listen to each other; how we feed one another. How we see people around us. How we work with them. Fairness is a tributary of love; so is justice. If we love the world, the life we are given, the most loving thing we can do is to share it with others, to ensure all people have equal access to this world. Our nations often behave like dysfunctional parents, dividing and chivying up the world, playing us off one another. Part of being a citizen is rejecting this model and learning to love outside it. Breaking the cycle of stingy nation-states that seem to need more and more love but are less and less able to give it to their citizens.

It's not just our nations letting us down, though. Much of our culture is structured around a similar model of love migrating only upward. A famous person by definition is someone adored by millions, someone who always needs more love. One of the most common things children say they want to be when they grow up is famous. What does this mean? Have we created a machine of a culture that bleaches love down to its mineral content? That sells and transports it like a commodity? Why are we so addicted to this synthetic form of love? We have built up an entire system of interacting with each other that mimics the forms of media that revolve around this model of giving and receiving stripped-down love in the form of attention. Of winners and losers in the stakes of love. Of oligarchs of this fake love.

If we are lucky, though, all of us remember what real love feels like. It involves food, and touch, and laughter, and acknowledgment. It is the opposite of loneliness. We have been trying to translate this feeling through a screen, and it is simply not possible, especially when the feeling is disseminated among so many people. The opportunity to give love, though, lies in wait all around us. We can often touch the very people to whom we can give more freely. And virtually everywhere one lives, there are visitors, there are people in need. There are those who are dying of thirst, dying for love. All our prophets, whatever religion one belongs to, spoke of the necessity of loving the weak, the needy, the overlooked. We need only give to realize that doing so makes giving more possible. The love that sees the corner of a lunchroom, where a child sits alone. The love that calls the home of the overlooked and expresses concern. The love that gives a blanket to a person sleeping on the street. The love that has weapons it does not use. We do not have to adopt the language of war to realize how revolutionary love can be. If we were to indulge in this kind of love—warm, indiscriminate, passionate love—in our lives, the tyrannies we face could not control us, any more than one person could stop a river from flowing downhill.

Monument

When we die, we lose everything: our bodies, those we love, all the riches we can accumulate in this brief life. Most of us also lose our names. Our names crackle like the snakeskin out of which we will crawl into the next life. Unless, of course, we have done terrific or terrible things. Then our names linger behind, free of our gravestones, a coin one can tender for stories. She did this, he did that, they believed in freedom, they were burned alive . . . Occasionally cultures seek to game this erratic silting of the dead from the living. So they put up a monument.

Far too many of the monuments are to killers. If you see a statue of a soldier on horseback with sword raised, the man it celebrates killed a great many. If the horseback rider is surrounded by men, his death toll often runs into the thousands. Rarely are the killers women, even though we know they, too, are sent to war. There are monuments to generals who died like martyrs and to unknown soldiers who perished invisibly. Bomber pilots, ship commanders, survivors of trench warfare, prisoners of war, scouts on horseback or off, the ones who patched them up, and the leaders who burned the midnight oil, souls afire in guilt and grief. Monuments glorify war.

And then we have everyone else. All the non-killers, the non-warmongers. The abolitionists, the inventors, the developers, the professors, the prosecutors, and the halfway-house homesteaders. The agitators for justice. Everywhere one goes, monuments look down on us, dragging their stories forward into our time. Telling us who sacrificed and what so we could be citizens. Take even a cursory glance at these statues and you get a strong sense as to whose debt matters, what kind of institutions need narratives, and what parts of the past aren't past at all. Some of this narrativizing isn't just offensive; it's a rearguard attempt to refight the unwon battles of the past.

All of us would like to believe civilization moves in a progressive line—from tyranny to freedom, from darkness into light. Monuments, however, tell a far different story. Decency swings like a pendulum in societies. On one end of its swing there's an expansion in the idea of citizenship, during which time we have monuments to civil rights leaders, givers, and those who fight for environmental protections. Then the pendulum swings the other way, and a society will begin to narrow the definition as much as possible. Say, to only white men. In order to narrow a society, leaders need to point toward figures of the past who have done the same thing. They always make it sound painful to be so unkind, but necessary. Unfairness becomes a kind of strength. And then these leaders point to those who lived, fought, and died for the idea of our nations. It helps in these moments to have monuments.

During this type of pendulum swing—the kind the whole world is living through—a light will suddenly be shone on the previously invisible figures of our past. The expellers. The killers. The unrepentant racists. The war criminals. The bigots and the thieves. Names that were unutterable will begin coming back. Their names will be resurrected, repolished, and sent back into circulation. The ear shocks at first. *Did I hear that?* one will think, listening to a public debate. *Yes, I did. There's the name again.* Suddenly, we'll begin to notice all the monuments of such figures standing amid us, seemingly dusty and unregarded for years. Why were they never taken down in the time of rights expansion? Chances are that the people who had the power to put up and take down monuments didn't feel the need, because it wasn't their lives under offense by such monuments. Or public apathy: who cares about that dead old thing one walks by on the way to work. In fact, what such monuments have been doing is waiting for their reanimation.

In some countries that have seen war, parts of their well-known cities are left as they were at war's end. Hollow-eyed buildings stand in haunting darkness. Bullet-scarred storefronts sell fresh bread. This is how we remember—not by suppressing the parts of our history in which we acted shamefully but by keeping it present. Enfolding these dark times into the narrative of nations so that hopefully no one should ever assume a nation is built by love alone. It takes violence to make a nation. And also, violence always threatens to tear nations apart.

Many other things make a nation, though. Teachers, nurses, dockworkers, and showroom clerks. Ministers, bus drivers, grandmothers, and carpenters, too. The most expansive definition of a nation we can create is one that says all the people living within a geographic area—and those who claim it from afar, based on its shared values—make a nation. Our leaders would never willingly agree to it, though, because such a definition would distribute power far too equally, and make war seem far too foolish. If one nation is not substantially different from another, and we are made of the same kinds of people, why go to war? Why celebrate killing? Why expel people from our borders when we know many of them make economies stronger? Why build all those monuments?

Monuments need to celebrate killing, then, because the turn of time tells us to forget. We live, we die, we are forgotten. There is a comfort in this, as each new generation gets a chance to be better to each other. We are given new tools, new laws, new devices, new infrastructure, new discoveries of science, new clues to the combined and complicated origins of humankind. We know what these enlarging elements are because they have enriched us all: the scientists who found the cure for polio, the builders who erected public libraries, the orators who called out for freedom and fairness in dark times.

What if our monuments spent as much time bringing individuals like these and their stories back into our present?

What if we had more monuments to poets, painters, ornithologists, glassworkers, comedians, physicians, and educators, too? What if they stood in public squares looking down on unpacked lunches and loomed over public parks, giving silent example?

What if our monuments did a better job remembering our dark times? What if instead of keeping figures of hate standing dustily on street corners, we found ways to remember what such figures did? The controlled starvation of scores of populations. What if every place a lynching happened was marked in some way? Some of these ways of remembering are beginning to become formalized; justice doesn't happen in one's own lifetime. The quest for it carries forward into the next generation, and if we can remember ethically, our monuments to cruelty won't come back from the dead.

Especially if we find a way to rethink what kind of

person winds up on a monument. What if our monuments had more to do with truly forgotten people? What if exceptional people weren't memorialized in town squares, but decent people were? If instead of walking by statues of people who often left their families so they could make a name for eternity, we saw more statues of the people who stayed at home? The grandmother who took care of her grandchildren so her daughter could work the late shift at a hospital to find a cure for Bells' palsy. The uncle who moved into a family home because he developed a motor-neuron disease and who played cards with his niece and nephew and taught them the incurable optimism of humor.

What if our official history had a bit more to do with the lives of the people who lived through it? Would we need so many monuments? Would it be possible to erect statues of killers at all, or generals who so clearly stood for hate? What if all these statues that stood for such terrible things—and we know what they are—were ripped up all over the world and in the holes each one left behind trees were planted? Isn't it possible in years those trees would grow and arc over the pavement around them, creating a circle that is cool in the summer and bursting with color in the fall. Reminding everyone who sits beneath them, in ways far kinder than a general with sword raised, that our time is limited—asking, How do you want to spend it?

Norms

Societies need norms just as much as they require laws—even those run by parliamentary governments, in which norms become the laws. Norms are manners writ large. A law says you must; a norm says you ought. This is the way we do it. Each time someone enacts a norm, she reminds us of the gap between legislation and behavior. She also affirms the ability for a society to police that gap among itself. A society that legislated every aspect of civil life would trust nothing to human decency. And yet the history of any society teaches that legislation does not always bend toward the arc of justice. Also, some norms are cruel. For instance, prior to Jim Crow laws, it was simply the norm to treat people of color as subhuman; with their passage, it became the law.

And so legislation needs to intervene when norms are monstrous. It has been the norm to beat women; it has been the norm to work children to death; it has been the norm to enslave people; it has been the norm to look the other way when members of the church abuse young children; it has been the norm to treat female desire as dangerous; it has been the norm to allow only opposite-sex couples to display affection in public; it has been the norm to treat female employees as sexual objects; it has been the norm for many cultures to project their fears upon black bodies; it has been the norm to discourage women from pursuing intellectual education; it has been the norm to carry guns; it has been the norm for men to do all the talking; it has been the norm never to enter a doorway before a woman or a child younger than eight. It has been the norm not to speak of money.

Norms tell us as much about a society as its culture does, the latter often dealing with fantasies and nightmares. By contrast, norms track the status quo, and by and large reinforce it. Over time, especially in informal societies and those with yawning inequalities, the status quo becomes a kind of pejorative—as it should. But some parts of the status quo are necessary; tactical norms, or manners, formalize decency. They tell us how to act in social situations and in so doing lubricate interactions and create a shorthand for kindness. Furthermore, reality is by nature chaotic; some agreement on what is real, tangible, and true is absolutely necessary for any society to function. In this way, small-scale norms and manners make a society; they render it readier to function.

Many tyrants have rightly discovered that the swiftest way to undercut a civil society is to flaunt its norms. Coups are dangerous and costly; revolutions take time. Turning a society upon itself by destroying its norms can be done rapidly in our digital age. Why? Every time a citizen enacts a norm, a small, perhaps mostly inaudible internal voice is suppressed. One that says, I, I, I. One that brags. One that stomps and chants for its own liberty. Sadly, many of the most powerful citizens in societies have to unlearn bigotry; they have to be educated into seeing their privileges—the point where their entitlement meets the disenfranchisement of another. A psychic undercurrent of resentment will always run beneath a society attempting to do this delicate disarming of its powerful few. Many societies that see themselves as having a color problem, an immigrant problem, an issue with any single group, in fact have a bigger problem with power: as in, those who refuse to give it up, share it, or simply put aside their ability to hurt people and not call it sadism.

A highly visible person who exults in the flaunting of norms can be an explosive figure in this environment. With a few powerful strikes against norms, he can tap into that undercurrent and agitate it forth. The force with which such resentment geysers up in cultures ruled by norms will be mistaken for a revolution. It may even feel like social change. But the spouting river of resentment is neither; it's simply the released pressure of vandalized norms. In societies that have had a status quo, there's a deranged pleasure in this moment, just as there's a more innocent happiness in being caught in a sudden and torrential downpour.

But a tyrant destroying norms isn't the weather; he's often *making* the weather. Societies that have had a status quo are especially prone to confusing the two. As the chattering classes seek to diagnose this sudden shift in climate, the aspirational tyrant meanwhile gleefully swings another sharp ax, cutting at another norm.

We have been living through such an extraordinary period in recent years. A great many underground streams, creeks, and, yes, rivers have been unleashed with a few key performances of mendacity. And now, as we stand about in a landscape raining with the unleashed resentments of the powerful, our governments are exploiting the chaos to consolidate even more control. It is a bizarre and stressful time period for everyone, but especially those who saw it coming. The arcs of norms always pivot too easily upon the treatment of the weak, of anyone who isn't considered normal, of the people a society designates as "less than" so that it can define its citizens by subtraction. The demolishment of norms does not often lead to kinder ones; it can lead all too quickly to a return to lethal ones. The civil rights era of the 1960s, for instance, gave way to the mass incarceration of the 1970s.

One of the bewildering moods of our present moment revolves around the way culture, chaos, and tyranny can seem immune to ridicule. Comedians, the best of them, after all, function in this space—exploding norms that have become so sacred they are unsayable. Satire always turns its flames toward the coals of a society's absurdities, many of which are contained in its norms. There's often a lot of heat trapped in there. Cultural figures who produce such art are necessary, and sometimes live outside the rules of society so that they can jest about it. Societies need these artists so dearly that they desperately try to bring them into the fold, and in so doing, normalize the critique.

When someone who functions like a comedian or a satirist—skewering or demolishing norms in public—manages to secure the centers of power, one would think revolution would be the result. In fact, with the right vectors of political power, a society's response often mimics its treatment of those dangerous comedians. It tries to normalize such a person. To build a coherent new sense of reality by enfolding this agent of chaos into its view of itself. One can especially watch this happening with autocrats. First, their photograph begins appearing everywhere—as if we might forget they exist were we not reminded of them. Then the commentariat builds a kind of intellectual scaffolding. And then the old guard of normative culture embraces them. Even if it's briefly. By this point, the person could have amassed the power of an actual tyrant—and it will be too late to joke him offstage.

Optimism

Hope is like the oxygen to optimism's fire. Without it, optimism can never break out, and then we truly live in the dark. Optimism is not a form of naivete; it's a necessary wedge of anticipation. Hope says to us, It would be nice if this happened; optimism replies, with its flicker of light, I really think it might. In that regard, hope is an intimate and personal emotion, nurtured in the small hours. It can be grown like a nightshade. By reading poetry, listening to music, baking by oneself, or watching one's child sleep. Walk to a shoreline and see the ways birds fish, and you may return with hope. Go to a protest and walk amid other bodies standing up for decency, fairness, and justice, and you will return with optimism.

A true tyranny will try to smash hope and optimism at the same time. You can hear it in the messaging. Some of it will target groups who agitate for justice, and some of it will simply be strange, cruel, and barbaric rhetoric. A tyranny will try to flood the zone of our attentions, so that everywhere we turn, it's all we see. Altering, arranging, and filtering reality toward its favor. You can feel this most acutely in the body. Immigration and policing and military intervention are not actually important to tyrannies philosophically; these are just the ways they can legitimately begin to express and project power. As a tyranny begins to rise, the language will turn violent. Then it will encourage violence. Then it will applaud violence. Then it will start to claim the right to violence. How violence is necessary. It will test the waters with missile strikes, calling in the national guard, military parades. Meanwhile, its shock troops, the ones that operate on the intimate, secretive level, will turn their force onto the weak and precarious. Picking them off. Deporting them, beating them, or simply killing them.

In most societies, this kind of low-level barbarism has been happening for years. It either hasn't been filmed or has been so selectively practiced upon the marginal that these societies have never had to deal with the cruelty of their law enforcement. Once a tyranny arises, though, especially when driven by the destruction of norms, there will be a push to erode this cloak of secrecy and shame. In empires, a merging will occur in the language used to describe internal and external errands of force. As if places need to be tamed, like frontiers. We will begin to realize that our internal police forces look a lot like armies; they are weaponized like brigades; they regard people in the areas they patrol as the enemy.

In such an environment, optimism is as dangerous

to the powerful as a wildfire. Have you ever watched a wildfire being fought? When it is big enough, it must be battled from above and from within. The firefighters doing this work often put their lives in danger to ensure separate blazes never, ever join. Tyrannies take a similar approach to optimism. If optimism stays within a sector of society or within a group, it is easy to fight. You dump on it from above and surround it from below. If no other fire is able to join it, that kind of optimism can be extinguished, or at least severely contained.

But when fires join, they become incredibly difficult to put out. So when victims of school shootings join hands with communities scorched by gang violence and agitate for change, that is a blaze of optimism. When women who have been preyed upon and men who have been assaulted by other men find their common ground, that is a formidable fire. When women of color and gay men march together, using their bodies to demonstrate for justice, that is a column of optimism. If the neglected elderly see brothers and sisters in shabbily treated war veterans, that is an inferno of optimism; most societies spend a huge portion of their budgets on those two populations. You will note a tyranny by how they attempt to divide and isolate populations. Douse them with flattery.

Only in a society that practices some vigilance about how language is used will this kind of aerial praise not feel like water. It will work instead as an accelerant. Here's why hope can do more than just flicker in the dark. Hope can be practiced in monitoring. A tyranny spreads through mendacity; almost no one would willingly agree to a tyranny from the start. Tracking those lies, the deformations of language, ordering and displaying them, often requires more time than any institution or any one individual has—this is why protests in times of power abuse feel so good, why agitators need the light of optimism they create. The bulwarking of reality one must sustain in such times takes effort and energy. Join a crowd of people who have been doing the same—tracking and ordering lies like you—and one doesn't simply encounter like-mindedness; there will be a similar vibration on a cellular level. It will feel like music.

Protests are just one way to agitate such blazes to light, though. Like aerial firefighters, governments have become very good at controlling such resistance. How to steer, contain, control, and ultimately extinguish them. What they can't deal with are hundreds and hundreds of little fires breaking out simultaneously. This is why resistance to a nationalized tyranny is best begun at a small level. Pouring one's hope, such as it exists, into local institutions. Going to your council meeting, voting in local elections, getting to know your neighbors, shopping locally, defining and defending fairness with people whose actual faces you can see—and if they don't agree with you about how to treat fellow human beings, arguing with them for those values.

We have neglected these nearer worlds. Those of us who live in cities and those of us who reside in small towns. We have been sold and bought into an idea of digital freedom and consumer life that depends on isolation and detachment. Even when it's pitching us connection. Shopping from afar and even overseas for better prices. Chatting with strangers across the globe. Using satellites to navigate. You don't need Google Maps if you know the streets around you. You don't need to tell neighbors you checked in at the local diner if chances are someone there will later tell your friends. You don't need to post a comment on a screen and look for likes; if you speak up in a local council meeting, people will respond immediately.

Here's one big secret about this way of living we have all too easily forgotten. It feels good. Not everyone is friendly, of course, and you can't do it in the dead of night, but being known, being part of a group, even if it's randomly assembled through accidents of employment, birth, or marriage, feels good. These small groups are very difficult to stop, too, if many of them are active at the same time. If they chimney hope, and adjacent groups can see fires burning near them. Gradually, the terror dream that tyrannies often unspool for their populations across the media will be revealed for what it is: a giant form of narrativized distraction.

Forces within culture will try to participate in this distraction tool—to scoop from its well of water. In times of rising tyranny, these forms of culture may even seem a tiny bit like resistance, because they arrive with the feel of familiarity. In our moment, apocalyptic fantasies are all the rage, even as our governments are participating in making them come true—especially when it comes to the environment. Sea levels rising; no one listening to scientists; here come the waves; there goes the Statue of Liberty. How many times has that movie been made? Perhaps the fact that it can all be beaten back by one man and a dog with good swimming skills lets us off the hook too easily?

A thousand zombie films won't help what ails us, however. Or superhero films. Or cli-fi films. These kinds of high-budget escape will eventually envelop us in a voluptuous apathy that will allow us to go down slowly, all while being entertained. When we feel this enchantment becoming an indulgence, it is time to turn off the televisions and our binge-watched shows and do the slightly harder work of lighting small fires. Of stocking optimism. This means leaving our houses; sometimes, it might even involve talking to people we aren't friends with on social media. It will be awkward, and it might even be a bit boring. But eventually, a spark might catch a cross breeze and lend flame to another community, one that also needs it, and that will light another. In time, if we are patient, this form of small-scale resistance will enable us to rebuild what we have lost—to interact with one another actually and not as forms of apocalyptic entertainment.

Police

We cannot live without law enforcement. Some people will simply break the law until stopped. So our societies must deputize some people to stop, detain, and arrest those who are flaunting the law. With force on occasion and lethal force in very rare instances. In this way, the police should be the handmaidens of justice. Many people become police officers in order to be just that. In societies tipping toward tyranny, however, the police begin to act more like iron maidens. The permission to use violence draws out job applicants who want to use force, or have preconceived notions of who to use it on. Patrolling our towns and cities, unobserved or simply unaccountable—as very few police officers are ever indicted for, let alone convicted of, murder—they have done horrific things to innocent people.

Over the past decade, as mobile phones were updated with video cameras, the cruelty most communities of color have experienced was exposed to a white audience. Throughout the world, but especially in the United States, the police have not always been enforcing the law. They have often been enacting racialized cruelty and death sentences upon the bodies of black and brown citizens. There is no decency here, no justice, and very little cause for optimism. Just obvious, vicious racism entitled by a badge. Boys shot in grocery stores, parking lots, playgrounds. Men stopped and shot before they had a chance to raise their hands. Men on the ground, shot for moving; men on the ground, shot for not moving. Mentally ill men shot for being disturbed. Men choked to death for selling cigarettes; women tackled for driving with a broken taillight. In 2018, the police in America killed almost one thousand people. On average, one police officer is killed per week.

One thousand to fifty—any general would call that a bloodbath. And we're watching it happen. Indeed, now we're even seeing it live, sometimes, as a man bleeds to death in his own car. How has U.S. society not tipped into full-blown revolt? Thirty years ago, one video of police brutality caused a riot that cost scores of lives. Now, we see one such video a day, sometimes more. The forces of tyranny have discovered something awful in aerated trauma. If they can move the public from shock to apathy, they can continue their behavior unheeded—which is precisely what has happened in America. The videos of John Crawford and Tamir Rice and Walter Scott being killed caused shock, alarm, and massive protests. The resistance movement Black Lives Matter arose through this trauma and gave birth to splinter groups that watch and report on police brutality, organizing protests and more in the aftermath of killings. Freeways were closed by bodies marching to agitate against these abuses. Spectacles of solidarity were created in high-end shopping plazas and train stations. Bodies of all colors lay down for justice.

Yet how much has been changed?

It is the ethical responsibility of white people to attend such protests because the killing is often done in their name. That is the only way it can be rejected: for whites to put their bodies in harm's way, too. The police understand, however, that apathy can be more powerful than the call of conscience. Especially for the comfortable. And so the police have waited out the protests, allowing the voices of protesters to be heard, to be lodged, slowly funneling the marchers into smaller and smaller public spaces until they must disperse. Law enforcement has done the same thing on a metaphorical level. Waiting out the novelty of a protest movement until the comfortable, the curious, and the—let's face it—white people have been splintered off. Then Black Lives Matter and movements like it become protests driven by people of color. This is a fire that can be fought from above and around. It can be contained. And the powerful can watch on their televisions and consume their outrage and empathy as a form of entertainment.

And so five years after the spectacular killings of

Michael Brown and John Crawford, the police are killing just as many people of color as ever. The U.S. Justice Department's civil rights investigation into the behavior of police departments across a dozen cities was digested and then quietly put away by a racist attorney general. In fact, the Justice Department has decided its primary role should be to investigate the perversions of justice enacted upon white people in colleges and universities and in places where they are "discriminated against." More police shooting videos are aired than ever before, but now they must contend with the spectacles produced by an entertainer president. One who knows how ratings are king and how people always need something new. He also knows how easily people can be manipulated by their fears.

Here's one of the peculiar things about our present moment. It's considered more offensive to be called a racist than to exhibit racist behavior. All a person acting with conscious or unconscious racism needs to do to claim offense is to talk about fear. It was because of fear that a barista called law enforcement about two men sitting in a coffee shop waiting for a friend. Fear sends not one officer to speak to them, but *seven*. Fear means a dialogue about this event doesn't linger on the eight hours the two men had to spend in police custody for not breaking the law; it instead talks about crime and the reasons why a rational person *might* call law enforcement because two black men are waiting for a friend to have a discussion over coffee. They were being polite, these men, not ordering first. That and their skin color were their crimes. Fear instead says that the woman placing the call had good reason to act like a racist. Fear is the racist's fig leaf.

In a society whose norms are racist but whose laws are not always prejudiced, the police can act as a corrective. Here's one reason among many why who leads a country matters. If a president or a prime minister publicly encourages officers to rough up subjects, to punch or kick them, saying he will pay their legal bills, if he claims there are good people on both sides of a white-power rally that leads to the death of one protester, the message is clear to law enforcement: you can do anything. Thus in America the momentum has tipped toward enforcing racist norms. If you polled citizens, they might even feel a different way: that law enforcement should be fair and equal in policing the behavior of citizens. It doesn't matter. The police have an immense amount of power. When videotaped and broadcast episodes of abuse do not lead to convictions and punishment, the worst elements within the police will learn the lesson coming from the top. You can operate with impunity. This message can only lead to corruption, too: some people like physical violence; others, economic violence. Some of them will take and extort. They are not different people from citizens, the police: some of them will do this until they are stopped, and if they are not stopped by the law, they need to be stopped some other way.

In an ideal world, one reason the federal government exists in many places is to police the passions of regions. If parts of a country try to restrict the voting rights or civil rights of citizens, the federal government should step in to enforce a correction. Once tyranny has risen to the top, to the federal level, however, the federal government cannot be trusted and change needs to be led from the bottom. Communities can hold their own police accountable by protesting, by bringing civil suits against them in some countries, by shaming them sometimes, by naming them the way victims are named. Change can also be achieved through positive action, by creating opportunities for dialogue. We cannot depend upon the enlightened within police forces to lead this charge; most police departments have a culture of collective protection.

It would be better if the police knew the people they were protecting. What if more local councils called for community policing so that officers responding to calls about petty burglary, or noise complaints, or a mentally ill person acting erratically in public had a good chance of knowing the people they were talking to? If they knew the environment? What if the officer called to a coffee shop in Philadelphia knew the barista? What if he knew the men sitting there? A lot of people's time and energy would not have been wasted, and two men would not have been humiliated in public. This sounds like a small thing, but there can be life-and-death permutations to community policing. In the case of Alejandro Nieto, shot on a park bench in the San Francisco neighborhood where he grew up—but a stranger to the two white men who called the police on him, and also the police who responded to the call—he'd still be alive. Each time an incident like this occurs, the trust between the police and the community is set back a generation. If your sister or brother were shot, what would you do? What would you feel when you saw that uniform?

The police need to do more than act in good faith to repair these wounds. They need to become part of the community. Too many police drive in from miles away to patrol a neighborhood that is not their own. What if they were seen more often out of uniform; what if they were seen in the places believers go to practice their faith? What if their kids went to the same schools? What if these same police officers held pancake breakfasts rather than peered out of slow-moving patrol cars? What if they helped organize fund-raisers for institutions other than themselves—institutions the community cared about, such as schools, hospitals, parks, and cultural spaces? What if some of the poets who write about the cost of police brutality were invited into precincts to talk to the police? What if the police saw this as an investment in their own safety? A great many police departments spend huge amounts of money, especially in America, on paying off civil lawsuits. Why are they willing to spend in the aftermath but not in the present tense?

What if more police were courteous?

In some cities, it is virtually impossible to speak to an officer who is friendly. Ever ask one for directions and hear, *Do I look like a map?* Is this what a public servant should sound like? Is it too hard to hire and train friendly people? Let alone people who look like the population they're going to police? Even collection agents are friendlier. How about this as a bare minimum, then: an ability to project kindness alongside the authority to protect. Are these two things truly at odds? What if small and disparate acts of kindness could lead in some zigzagged way to hope, even when it's not being led from the top? Wouldn't that be more preferable to this? To riding along in bulletproof vests wearing body cams? To glancing up at people looking back at you with distrust, dressed for a war? To watching this tedious, disgusting show?

Questions

Questions are the respiratory system of children. Every breath they take brings in the world, expanding them, then out comes the response. Another question. It's how children build the world, interrogate it, understand it. At some point, like some strange being that first breathes with gills, then with lungs, most of us stop absorbing the world this way. We switch to our own voices; reacting in, reacting out. A few professions allow people to continue to ask questions: journalists, researchers, detectives, and philosophers ask questions. But most of these jobs—save for philosophy—presume the questions can be answered. Meanwhile, grow old enough to become one of these professional question-askers, and you will always be humbled by the average four-year-old. The scope of their questions is enormous, constant, unstrange to them. Radical.

We need to learn how to keep asking questions. QUESTION EVERYTHING is a bumper sticker you commonly see in California. REMEMBER QUESTIONS? might be a better one. A question can come in any size. Where are we going today? can be put in your breast pocket. How do you feel? might require a pants pocket. Why do we all act as if the news is the one main story? is going to need a backpack. If we learn to ask one another small questions, we can begin to see each other a bit better. Where are you coming from? How was work today? How is your family? Learning to ask questions is essential to basic decency. A question says, I don't just see you, but I also know there's more to what I see. Have you ever sat with someone who doesn't ask any questions? It's stunning.

Yet as we get older, and the world is named, and bodies are categorized for us by culture, and we learn all the responsibilities that come with citizenship, we start to repel the world. There's enough world for us, or so we think, and so we practice apathy. We travel through the world in envelopes of independence disguised as envelopes of freedom—the car, the internet—and we pack up and put away our questions. We keep, if we are lucky, the ability to raise polite inquiries. But about the rest? Life is too busy for that. Too complex. Too obviously unfair. Do we really want to know about the rest? Let alone someone else?

And so daily agitation becomes a kind of armor. We may not see it as apathy; it might feel like privacy, or dignity, or realism. Yet when we enter the world without questions, we are essentially accepting the universe at face value—or saying, It might as well do, because I cannot change it. This is dangerous. When large parts of a culture operate this way, society becomes nihilistic. It can turn decadent. It tips toward pornography, or the repetition of once-improvisational acts with diminishing pleasure. Much of the entertainment industry in the West revolves around fulfilling such needs. Like all forms of genre, these types of escape meet our expectations; they do not require much of us. We sit or even stand and see them. We can watch them on our phones on our way to work. By the end, we know something will have happened, maybe something surprising.

One of the main problems with questions of all sizes is they require the possibility of change. A willingness to change. Activism is in essence a way of life that commits to questions: What if all these workers were paid more? How would our country look if corporations paid the same tax rate as people? Why do we elect representatives more beholden to entities than to human beings? *Activism*—a word so often maligned because it is deeply threatening to power—is a way of asking big questions that lead to practical questions: How are our elections structured? Whose money enters them? What bill made that funding structure possible? Who voted for that bill? How many people in that representative's district lost their jobs because of corporate support for that bill? How many of them want to come to a rally? What are the obstacles to these people giving up their time to do so? How do we get around them?

Human civilization is based upon a balance between questions and answers. The best civilizations create structures that allow citizens not just to ask questions; they channel the power of their questions. Elections, schools, libraries, newspapers, public squares, and carnivals are question-driven. In decadent societies, in those stumbling toward tyranny, the parts of culture that foster and develop questions come under threat. Journalists, scientists, schoolteachers. Anytime you hear someone at a microphone railing against these citizens, be wary. Even more so if they are in uniform. In wartime, you are not supposed to second-guess the government. Tyrannies try to create rhetorical structures of wartime by dreaming up false and sometimes even vague binaries. You are either with us or against us. Who is *us*? If you have to ask, you are not one of us.

A citizen is a person who asks questions of their government. A citizen asserts their right to ask; a subject has to ask for the right. Many of us live in societies where the elected or so-called elected leader would like many of us to have to beg for the ability to ask a question. Have you ever watched television interviews in a dictatorship? They are unintentionally hilarious. Tell us, fearless leader, how does it feel to be so loved? How are you enjoying your election victory? You can deduce the health of a society by how rigorously it questions those in power. It may be a performance, but Prime Minister's Question Time in the U.K. serves an important symbolic purpose: it says that the leader of a nation is not above being grilled and is expected to have answers.

When a society stops asking questions upward, it often turns the nascent questioning energy upon itself. This is a mistake. Are you not, sir, a fraud and a racist? should not be anyone's first question of the day. Not simply because it turns us into characters in a cheap thriller but rather because it narrows the type of question we ask into a rhetorical trap. If we ask only implicating questions, are we really asking questions? We need to begin small, really small, to remember how many ways there are to ask a question. Would you like some coffee? What's in the newspaper? What is the weather today? How would you like the day to go? Why do you have to stay late? When do you want to talk about looking for a job? Who can help you with that?

If we ask questions across, up, and down the register, of different sizes and with all types of sharpness, our lives feel less static. They take on a shapeliness that can, in the best moments, feel like optimism. If we move beyond rhetorical questions and implicating questions to open-ended questions, we realize our lives are only as small as the questions we ask. In some moments, the right questions can prompt an untold story. In others, a well-timed inquiry may force us to contend with what we are: not who we wish to be, or imagine ourselves to be, but how we are living in the world today. If we have not contended with this gap between what we are and what we wish to be on a societal level, we are open to all kinds of manipulations—candidates can speak to our fears rather than our realities. Let alone our hopes. They can present themselves as the answer to an unasked question.

We all know that even in love, even in the most intense and long-lasting romantic love, one person cannot be the answer to our problems. So how could a leader be? Would any of us accept a loving relationship in which one person said to the other, I alone can make you whole. That usually ends in tears, or worse. When a leader such as this appears, we have often long since stopped asking questions. And yet it is never too late. We are never too far gone to use small and big questions to unbury ourselves from a hole that apathy has filled in. We simply have to understand that digging is not necessarily what questions are for: it is, however, what they can do. We have made the mistake of thinking that the most powerful spade in our tool kit is the self: the I. On social media, in personal exploration, we have tried to excavate with it.

A question, however, a big question, gradually shrugs off the I. For a big question to get off the ground, it needs to open up a possible field of answers that is far bigger than one individual can contain or grapple with. This is why novels are such powerful dreaming devices: What if, they say, as we begin to read, what if this were you? In the best of them, you can almost hear the scaffolding falling away and the interrogative field opening up, possibly as big as space itself. All kinds of imaginative activity operates this way. Daydreaming is a way of asking ourselves questions; playing music, drawing, praying. It is in fact essential to prayer: What if someone or something were listening?

As we ask questions, the world's structures take on a whole different hue. If we ask, What if? often enough in our private lives, we may begin to do the same in our public lives. If the answers our structures return to us do not suffice, we may begin to question the structures themselves. Or we may begin to ask different questions. What if an election wasn't about who will best lead us but about who we are? What kinds of questions would we ask of our leaders? What if we required them to ask us questions in return? What if we demanded that candidates commit to protecting our ability to ask these questions? What if we had a right to an answer? What would our societies look like then? Who would we be?

Rage

Rage is a by-product of inequalities of power, just as carbon dioxide emerges from combustion. It fumes and clouds the sky. Burn something or someone, and there it plumes, rage, like a sign of action. Evidence of momentum. In fact, rage is the opposite; rage is the toxic by-product of what happens when anger has not led to action or change. A riot is an expression of rage, as is a tweet, vandalism, and drive-by hatred of any form. Let alone killing. A lynching was ultimately an expression of rage. Racists could kill or maim wantonly in the American South and yet never erase blackness, let alone the essential entwinement of African Americans' trauma and the existence of the country. This fueled a rage that still burns today. It has taken root in the very pinnacle of U.S. government again.

It should be said that rage feels good—to those who are in its possession. Rage is the release of trapped energy and tension, after all, as in comedy. As in any form of combustion. But whereas comedy can veer toward mirth, or even the transformative complexities of glimpsing a shared absurdity—whether it's in marriage or life under a tyrannical regime—rage doesn't see the other. So rage doesn't make that enlarging moment possible. Rage knows only the need for combustion, and for that reason, rage needs something or someone to burn. To destroy. That often means an enemy, even if it is the low-fuel flammable of straw men. Societies caught in cycles of stasis—where nothing is getting better—are especially prone to elevating people who create these straw men. At the very least, they give people something to burn. It doesn't matter what, so long as the rage can burn. On a very basic level, it's important for the group from which it comes to see this rage: they feel less alone.

Of course some forms of rage are more socially acceptable than others. Rage tracks a society's norms, after all. White rage has for centuries been acceptable; all other rage has had to find ways to hide itself or channel itself. Women have had to find ways to sublimate or hide their rage; so have people of color. So have immigrants. Some outlets are more destructive than others. For women and men who channel their rage at the gym, it is a double-edged sword: Am I chiseling my body into an instrument of power or just another representation of how I'm supposed to look?

Holding on to rage, living with it, is dangerous, as it changes a person. Live with rage too long and one's mind will be altered, and the pathways that made other pathways and reactions available are burned down to the nub, no longer passable. It's why new generations are so important to social change, and why intersections of different cultures are important to their movements. Everyone's rage is different and burns out different faculties. If you spend time in diverse-enough groups, you can keep alive the possibility of borrowing aspects from another community that are perhaps depleted in your own. This is so important in all groups, families, offices, schools. Anger builds up and layers, and leads to rage, and the rage born of this frustration can exhaust, even as it is born out of exhaustion. The relationship between many communities and the police is a perfect, justified example.

Populism of all stripes feeds on rage; it is what populist leaders activate in socially static and unfair societies. Change, true change, is so much harder; very often it seems impossible. So rage is the only thing the disempowered seem to have—the only social capital, the only electoral power. Not far off from that of a mob. The collective expression of rage can be intensely illuminating, it can be terrifying, but since it so often requires an enemy, and burning that enemy flattens an environment—purifies it briefly, which is the fallacy—rage ultimately destroys the larger possibilities on which citizenship depends. Once populism has begun to feed on rage, it has a hard time switching to a different accelerant. Populism scorches and scorches with the idea that ultimately a new, "purer" type of nation can be born or returned to. This is the triumph of tribalism.

There are more sustaining fires in our lives. In the middle of white-hot tribalism, though, they may not be apparent. But after rage has burned down enemies, after it has been turned again on the population themselves, after it has been revealed for what it is—a destructive force always pointed at something or someone—these smaller fires become apparent. Moments of decency reveal them; so can love. One of the things we hope for from leaders, that we in fact crave, is a demonstration of the possibilities beyond rage. The power of kindness and compassion. Of transforming hope into optimism. Otherwise a nation is always eating the rage coming from above, which can poison a country.

This means, on occasion, that the most effective thing a citizen can do is turn away from the powerful and their projections. To swivel away from rage in all its forms, when possible. This is not apathy, but rather a choice to direct attention toward less-destructive forms of heat and agitation. Many of these lights can be found off the internet, in the real world, where our bodies are more finely tuned instruments of empathy than our eyeballs and fingers.

Retuning ourselves from rage will take time, though, because in societies polarized by decades of its use, expressions outside this register have ceased to be heard or trusted. We have to ask ourselves the hard questions: Do we want to continue this way? At what point does this manner of illuminating debate lead to apocalypse? We have a terrible history, humans do, with change. So often not changing until we have to, or until we have destroyed something beautiful. Whales essentially were fished into extinction before we began to pierce the earth and extract the oil that has led to this current environmental crisis. In a similar way, weaning ourselves from rage in our current media climate is like switching from coal or oil to renewable power. We know we need to do this. Yet it is such a large-scale shift that enacting it means learning how to use an old and ever-present form of light. We have the ability, and that is what should give us hope. Biologically, mentally, we have evolved this capacity. If we can slow down, for the tiniest of moments, we can see a way through—using our imaginations.

R

Spirit

There was a time when the heart was our center. We spoke from the heart when we wanted to express our sincerity and intensity. We believed in something with all our hearts when it was a fundamental notion. We gave our hearts to our lovers because it meant holding out to them our essence—the all and everything of what we are. You searched your heart when it was a conscience you needed to consult.

In the centuries since neuroscience developed, though, we have shifted our lexicon from the heart to the mind. And from the mind very quickly to the language of machines. While the heart remains, we talk more and more of ourselves along the logic of computers and data. We use emojis rather than words; we deploy hashtags rather than references. We refer to the ways we're hardwired for justice or for resistance. We speak of deleting people from social circles when they have transgressed. Meanwhile, in public interactions we rely ever more on our own miniature pattern-recognition capacities—as if we can compete with the supercomputing power of our handheld devices—to know the world.

This is a dangerous development. We are not gadgets,

and operating like them ignores our greatest capacity—which is how to live in states of unknowing. Indeed, the scale of our ignorance is so gargantuan we have had to develop cultures to curate it. We do not know why we are here, so we developed religions to tell us stories about why; we do not know how we got here, so we created science to investigate the evidence; we do not know who we are, so we created governments to find ways of containing and organizing us and journalism to tell us how our experiments in living are going; we do not know what living feels like, it's so varied and complex, so we created the arts to show us, and they can thrive only when there is a mutual respect for the known and unknown quantities of life. We do not know how to store and access all these ways of knowing, so we created technology.

In times of rising tyranny, every single one of these forms of inquiry into our ignorance will come under attack. All so we can look to one power, sometimes even one person, for answers to our biggest questions. Indeed, tyrannical power systems will adopt the language of all these modes of knowing to signal to citizens that the wedge of insight each provides can be gleaned from only one source. In dictatorships, that means one ruler, reinforced by a police state; in capital systems, the market is often ascribed all the interrogative powers of all those ways of knowing. We are here to acquire things, say advertisements; what we think is determined by a market-like competition of ideas, and so on.

We do possess, however, another spade, another metaphor that can be used in times of distress, one that is perhaps more resilient than dictatorships and capitalist systems and can tell us a lot about how to deal with not knowing: that is the spirit. Speaking of the spirit is not a way to sideline the forms of knowledge described above; it's a way to contain everything these modes of knowing do not yet know. We speak of the spirit because we sense there's a part of ourselves that cannot be contained by our bodies, by our nations, by our lives, by our art. Sometimes, if you believe in the spirit, you simultaneously accept the spirit of another. That there's more to another person than their body, their behavior, their life. And very often this belief, however unfounded, leans toward the idea that a spirit contains the best of that other person.

The etymology of this belief is less interesting than the fact that it remains in cultures built by the Enlightenment and rational thought. Cognitive scientists have been studying brain waves and chemical shifts in the mind that take place when people undergo spiritual experiences. This is of course helpful information, and one day it may be used for the greater good, but it will not remove the need for a metaphor to contain our unknowingness, our best behavior, our essence in the scale of a reality too complex and too fast-moving for us to fully comprehend. That is how big the scale of our ignorance is and will continue to be. You can simultaneously not believe in God and recognize that we need this metaphor.

Consider, after all, some of the things we do not and perhaps never will know. No one can tell us where we were before we were born, and not a single person can tell us for certain what happens after we die. We are unclear as to how our universe was created, and we do not know what lies at the outer reaches of it. We have even had to dream up a concept—infinity—to contain the scale of this question, and the computational language of what exactly time is stands outside the capacity of most human beings. Finally, among other things, we know a fraction of what our environment knows, and all the life systems within it that call it home, and even though it's screaming to us in pain, agitating for relief as we kill off species after species, we do not know how to hear it.

The spirit is not a solution to these forms of unknowing but a prosthetic—just like technology—to deal with the fact that we need to live in the world among known and unknown things. Our ability to inhabit this in-between state is crucial to our justice system doing more than punishing. Only in novels can we fully enter the head of another, and so we think of the spirit. We live our lives, if we are lucky, in close proximity to people we can count on and put our faith in, and make assumptions about in times of joy and suffering. Others we simply live near to; and some we just pass on the street. In a world run by laws and norms, the notion of the spirit slips between these gaps and becomes, if you believe it, a way to put some faith in the capacity of the world for good.

There have of course been historical attempts to purify the spirit, to expel the spirit from the body, to treat the spirit like the only thing in us of value. Organized religion has too often veered into such campaigns. These cruelties and hysterias persist to this day, too, and are a blight on the possibilities a belief in the spirit holds. Very often these forms of abuse have been directed upon the most vulnerable people in our societies, and their suffering becomes a kind of spectacle through which the viewers are entertained and cleansed. It is a violation of the spirit to participate in these rituals, and modern life balances on a tipping point between the sadism of such tendencies and the optimism and decency that grow from an enlarged view of the spirit.

There are things we can do to lead with this enlarged spirit. To bring a spirited defense to citizenship and fairness to societies under threat. For starters, our rage to redeem and improve our world can be driven into hope and action if we respect the scale of our unknowing. The fundamental way of doing this is engaging in activities and pursuing actions that are exploratory in nature—asking questions of power, dreaming through life by reading, bolstering systems of education, respecting other people's bodies, and, most important, rejecting the purifying simplicities of tribalism.

One of the swiftest ways of activating the spirit is to give. Giving is the spirit's currency; apathy is its bankruptcy. Some of you reading this have probably once helped someone on a street and felt that peculiar raising of your arm hairs that occurs after giving time, love, energy, or resources to those in need. Even in the smallest gesture. The spirit does not always need permission to be engaged, but once it is, this enlarged spirit—this best-of-us spirit—rewards the body. It turns the body into an instrument for our best selves. It allows us to move in a world being reduced by our unknowing, our losses, by the monuments we erect to our certainties, and to make it larger, one action at a time.

Teachers

If our society is ever going to approach justice, we need revolutionary change, not just slow, incremental change. We need a return to enlarging principles and ideas, not a backslide into old hatreds. We need to begin addressing where inequality is born. Decency we can practice person to person. The environment we can help protect in day-to-day decisions—by eating less meat and using fewer fossil fuels. Addressing inequality, however, means looking at the structure of many of our societies themselves.

At the root of so many of our problems is our lack of support of public education and our dereliction of teachers.

If a person were to descend from Mars and learn how humans were compensated for the jobs we do, teacher salaries in most parts of the world would be a bafflement. Between the ages of four or five and eighteen, many children spend as much time with their teachers as they do with their parents. This is not just how our children learn, but also how they are socialized, how their bodies are cared for; it's where they see many of the models of adult life they will learn from, let alone the models of

T

care and love. Think for a second and you probably have a clear memory of the teacher who taught you at age six or seven. Whoever your child spends their hours with today will have a lasting impression, too.

Our early years are incredibly important. Cognitive scientists know that around age four, when kids are starting school, they begin to ask questions to intuit the shape and logic of the world. Anyone with a niece or a nephew or a child of their own will have answered such questions and marveled at their endlessness. Fielding this interrogation requires patience and a sense of humor. Almost all children have a sense of humor and respond well to jokes. Any good schoolteacher must have both a grasp of how children are and patience enough to enchant them into participation. It's so much easier to ignore them, and children eventually get the message. They will shut up, some of them. Make life a little easier—and worse. A neglected child, though, is one of the most unbeautiful things in the world.

It takes energy, work, and a peculiar form of calm to be around one child for long stretches of time—never mind thirty of them. One would want to hire exceptional people for this grueling and terribly important task. Now consider this: in many parts of the globe, we hand over the most precious people in our lives—our children—to a group of underfunded, hectored, overworked public servants who are so poorly supported that they often have to work second and third jobs to make ends meet. Meaning they return to work the next day and the next sleep-deprived and carrying ailments of the body that come with stress. Sometimes in an environment made dangerous by weapons.

Meanwhile, the CEO of a chemical company that produces carcinogen-laced pesticides will need two or three lifetimes to spend the money he or she makes.

How is this even remotely fair?

One of the mysteries of capitalism today has been the success with which it has made us all aspirational snobs. We don't want to take from the rich, in the event any of us wind up rich ourselves. It sounds like the kind of game a teacher would assign in schools to teach fairness. If you could possibly be rich, like monuments-to-your-name rich, but *possibly* poor by accepting the current system; or could go to a well-funded, enlightened, giving school and take your chances on the outcome, which would you choose? In this question, the risk being taken is one's own. Yet so many of us are willing to have our children take this risk themselves by reserving the right to pull them out of public schools.

An expensive school may lavish attention on children, but ultimately our kids grow into a world where many of the people they interact with, from nurses to bus drivers to accountants, let alone all the abstract members of the body politic, may not have shared such benefits. If you do not trust your child to public school but trust public water, what does that say? If you do not trust your child to public school but trust public transportation, what does that say? If you do not trust your child to public school but trust public elections to make decisions on how a nation is run, what does that say? Sadly, the answer to many of these questions may be that if you're well-off enough, the results of elections do not matter to you very much.

That has indeed been the case for a small but enormously powerful segment of many societies. For all the rest of us, the results have been devastating, as that sense of what is public, and how it needs to be curated, has been destroyed. One can clearly spot the devastation this model of public life has brought to the United States, especially in its private–public health-care system. Catastrophic health bills are now the number one cause of bankruptcy in America. The rich simply take their business elsewhere and indeed in the United States can purchase some of the best care in certain fields. The same is true in England.

Poor education is just as much a crisis, though its results take years, decades sometimes, to become apparent. The election of a willfully ignorant and gloatingly cruel president might be one such sign. Criminality is another. Loneliness. Suicide. The passage of an idiotic referendum sold on obvious lies. How about general political apathy? Indeed, societies need informed and educated citizens to function healthily. Without them, societies are prone to tribal control and mob mentality. That is precisely what one has been witnessing unfold in the United States and other parts of the globe.

It doesn't have to be so. Indeed, in America, as across a large part of the globe and in developing nations, the creation of mandatory public education was a remarkable thing. Bringing the United States from low literacy up to the present fueled the boom of postwar American life (that and entering World War II so late). By investing in physics, chemistry, and mathematics, the United States raised a generation of scientists who did extraordinary things, invented the internet, and cured seemingly incurable diseases. Graduates of public schools agitated for decency in our laws. Public schools, which once had strong arts and humanities programs, gave us Toni Morrison, Philip Roth, the founders of Apple and Google. But these facts are interesting only if we count on exceptional people to run the world. We need entire classes of people if we are to live in civil society. China is making this investment now. So is Germany, one of the best places in the world for a public education.

There has been a war on the practices and possibilities of government involvement in public life, and that approach to privatization has been exported from America around the world. This belief in the market above all else has not entirely toppled socialist democracies in Scandinavia, but it has been adopted elsewhere as nations have accommodated America's virulent form of late capitalism, including across England and in central Europe. Many of the former Soviet Bloc nations jumped straight to this stage of capitalism, meaning that at the moment of greatest possibility—when they needed their own Morrisons and Roths—they leapfrogged over mass literacy and education to breathtaking inequalities.

Svetlana Alexievich, the Belarusian Nobel Prize winner, tells the stories of life before, during, and after Communism; she was a product of public schools.

It serves the powerful to keep a society undereducated. An undereducated society is always more willing to overthrow facts, science, and even the role of journalism than one with a deep and profound sense of context. An undereducated society can be manipulated. An undereducated society will nurse resentments and paranoia that will make them prone to a tribal response. This is not to say all racists have gone to poor schools; in fact, the reality is quite the opposite. Some of the worst racists in our societies have gone to the best schools in our country. Racism, however, is a failure of education: if we did not segment our society so much by striating our children between private and public education, chances are that we'd have fewer racists.

It sounds preposterous, but it's possible to radically change our current crisis in education. It was once a point of pride to have gone to public schools. Then it became the norm to send one's children to private school in many societies; simultaneously, it became the law to underfund public schools. Real change will have to come from altering the norms and the law. We have to start by asking questions, publicly, privately, on all the forums we now go on to simply parrot and like or bark our latest slogan. What if we wondered aloud what would happen if teachers were suddenly given the same kind of salaries as doctors? After all, their effects are as deep and profound.

What if schools were given as much funding as corporations got in tax breaks?

What if each corporation paid a special school tax, just as they paid social security and health care taxes?

What if we spent as much on renovating school facilities as we did on producing weapons?

We have reached the limit of ways the internet and market-based solutions can improve public education; it is now clear that relying on both simply impoverishes the many for the benefit of a few. Indeed, if only a few hyper-rich products of public schools put their time and money behind a campaign to get the federal government and states to fund public schools properly, it's possible public schools might be, if not sexy again, then relevant.

Warren Buffett, after all, graduated from public schools. So did Amelia Earhart.

This doesn't mean replacing public funding for schools with private donations, but using outsider donors to lobby governments to increase their support of public education. Sadly, that's the reality in our time. The obvious needs to be stated. Indeed, in America, students have to walk out to resist the right not to be shot in their classrooms. Imagine if we had a population educated enough to understand what a catastrophe that is. What if the American population understood that the way legislation has been written in fact puts them in harm's way? Imagine the kind of accounting that would take place. Now watch as the students who grew up fighting these idiocies try to force this one change in gun laws through. Imagine if we were helping them make the world around them better; imagine then what would be possible.

Usurp It is so tempting to want to usurp power in times of its abuse. Your side, if you see things in such terms, has been down so long. *If only* you had the reins yourself. All the things you'd right. All the bodies you could break in punishment. All the citizens you'd invite back into the castle keep. What feasts and what joy—the celebrations! Justice at last, and then what? How would you use the power then? Would it be fair to give a bit back to the people whom it had been stolen from? Yes, of course. Now, who would you jail? What monuments would you build now?

The danger of this thinking is, of course, that it simply reproduces the conception of power as a vector of compulsion. The power to force, to order, to take, to kill, if necessary. That's the apex of agency in this conception: to remove the agency of another. If we are to live with people unlike us, however, we need to redefine an enlarged sense of power. This kind of power includes, but is not limited to, compassion, love, generosity, and curiosity. Truth and reconciliation commissions that have helped mend terrible wounds in societies nearly destroyed by violence have found that next to transparency and accountability, these

U

other values are of equal importance. Otherwise we are loading the gun for another cycle of violence, or abuse, to continue.

We need to see the humanity in our enemies. If not, we do what some of them do to us: which is to diminish our humanness until it is okay to abuse us. This is how armies function. A fully grown human being does not usually have it in their capacity to kill. You must enable him, pre-excuse her. So armies entering war zones are fed stories, lies, and the worst kind of shorthand to dehumanize the enemy. If you knew the soldier trained in your sights was writing a letter home to his disabled brother, would you kill that person?

Many of our empires have been on war footing for decades now. Pouring the toxins of this kind of language into the bloodstream of their warrior classes, whipping it up to a froth in the body politic. It is useful in both places. Nations, all of them, need an other: how else do they define who they are not? This has been one function of anti-Americanism. Some of this thinking indeed stems from revulsion at U.S. foreign policy, its interventions, its war-mongering and hypocrisy. Indeed the rage our current balance of power creates is bound to spill over into action.

A softer side, however, simply develops as a resistance to ubiquity. If America is everywhere, in the culture and climate of nations the world over, many of those nations need to develop within themselves a response: here's why we're not American. Humor can be a form of decency: it acknowledges a shared situation and defuses some rage by seeing the truth in it, often by pointing out small details. Imagine if stand-up comics, rather than armies, were sent to foreign countries. Imagine if stand-up comics, rather than police, were sent into neighborhoods. What if stand-up comics, rather than diplomats, were called in advance of summit talks? We spend billions sending arms—what harm could come?

It says something about how much rehabilitation we must do to our optimism that this string of questions will seem absurd. Yet for decades most nations have been sending men in suits and arms back and forth to one another. What good has this brought us? Can you feel the kind of apathy that squirts into your brain stem as you even imagine that picture? We must change the question if we want a different answer to what civil society can do. As citizens, many of us have the right to create new spaces, and out of the modes of interaction that unfold there, better ways to conceive of civil society. More than a billion people gave up their privacy to do this on Facebook; then we discovered it was simply turning us into commodities.

There's another way. Culture, by nature, does not have to be for or against anything; even the term *culture war* betrays what constitutes the elements of a real culture. Would you say Dostoyevsky is for or against the Russian state? Is Virginia Woolf pro- or anti-choice? What does Niemeyer have to say about capitalism? How about Pavarotti's plans for gay marriage? These questions are absurd. It's like asking a hippo whom it plans to vote for, or a lightning bolt whether it turned off the dryer. In our world, however, in these times, no part of culture is allowed to simply interact: it's constantly stopped at the border and asked for its papers.

So many cultures do the work of tyrannies in advance of a tyranny's total control. They inform on one another; they eat the elders or the young; they run campaigns to purify themselves. They banish those who do not parrot the party line. They often do all this in the name of resistance. These are not the times, the argument goes in such moments, for weakness. We must define ourselves by proving what we are not. In doing so, however, a resistance can make itself a mirror of tyranny. A resistance can reinscribe its notion of power so that by the time it has reached critical mass, all it knows how to do is usurp.

The greatest defense against tyranny is a celebration of complexity. Tyrannies, after all, are attempts to reduce the human to certain containable components, all of them beholden to a party, a system, or just one person. If humans cannot be reduced, however—if they refuse to be flattened into data, camps, groups for or against—they cannot be so easily steered, managed, and manipulated. Holding on to complexity, and the forms of living and culture that celebrate this—from cities and their interdependence and diversity, to art forms like the novel—will preserve the dream functions necessary to keep asking questions. To turn the interrogative mode from Who is in power? to What will they, or we, do with it?

Vote A vote is the difference between a citizen and a subject. The powerful used to be able to say to all and sundry, You must; a vote says to the powerful, No, you must listen.

Thus begins, in many places, the modern world.

For a long time the powers that be have turned an ear toward the people—because every two to four years, those voters are waiting for them. Everywhere the vote has traveled, so has a sense of accountability. If you are greedy or corrupt or abuse your power or ignore the needs of citizens, there's a chance you will be voted out.

So there has been a move, from the very beginning of the vote, to restrict who has the power to use it—to plane down the realm of responsibility. From the beginning, in most places, it was just men with land who could vote; then it was just men; then it's all those men plus women. The history of many liberal democracies is this story—at least in part: the drive toward greater inclusion.

Now we are swinging the other way. Most of our societies are so top-heavy—literally crumbling under the weight of an oligarch class whose interests are vastly overrepresented—that the only way for them to function is to reduce or even cancel the vote. Were people to vote at higher percentages, power would lose. So the vote itself has to come under attack.

Some of these assaults are soft and accomplished through suggestion. A foreign power or even a candidate may put out that the vote is rigged, stoking the already understandable apathy. In many two-party systems, the candidates themselves play a game in debates, provoking just enough apathy to shave off voters from each other's total. These subtractions can be accomplished with targeted messaging, too.

Apathy, however, is not enough to keep the powers that be in their seats. So voters literally have to be removed from rolls. Those who haven't voted in years are scrubbed from voter rolls; new laws are passed to make it harder to vote—paperwork is needed, appointments required. These rules target poor and overworked people, minorities, and those who have an unhappy relationship with the law's surgical precision. Sometimes "accidents" happen: you turn up to vote and your name isn't on the rolls.

On it goes. Districts are drawn and redrawn, especially in America, to make it especially difficult for one of the parties to win. Both parties have used this tool. In some cases, the police are brought out: nothing turns some voters away from a polling center like two or three squad cars parked, lights flashing. False messages are spread about polling time, about laws. Polling stations are moved across town to someplace inconvenient. In one recent election, a candidate illegally installed cameras inside polling stations. In the worst cases, people are beaten, chased away. Called and threatened. The history of voter suppression is told through the bodies of citizens.

Voting isn't entirely fair; it's only a partially decent enterprise. Yet it's the best one we've created for channeling civic participation.

The very first responsibility that comes with a vote, then, ought to be the awareness that it needs to be protected and constantly improved. A great many people are handed the right to vote, and it never occurs to them that it will be taken away. This fact needs to be taught to children—who have an instinct for fairness—when they first learn history and government. Many schoolbooks ask teachers to present the right to vote as an arrival point, a destiny of civic society, when in fact the vote is simply an element allowing a civic society to function. You corrode the vote and hope will go dark.

Social scientists have found that in the absence of mandatory voting, some people will always need to be coaxed to the polls. They are old, or indigent, or depressed, or lonely, or apathetic, or just simply not engaged. They don't have a ride, or they are too busy; they aren't feeling well, or they have better things to do. So volunteers need to walk door-to-door to speak with them about upcoming elections. To agitate democracy to life. Imagine if instead of 55 percent of people voting, 90 percent did. Imagine if this were a celebratory part of every civics class taught round the world—children escorted by an adult or two around neighborhoods reminding people to vote, with no partisan agenda? What sort of accountability would a candidate face? Who can face down the civics equivalent of a Girl Scout cookie sale?

This kind of ceremony feels like just the beginning of a series of changes that could protect the vote. Any government that refuses to consider them is sending up a red flag. Why isn't voting mandatory? Why isn't registration automatic, say, when you get a driver's license or a state ID? Why isn't voting a national, state, and local holiday with required paid leave? Why isn't public transportation free on voting days? Why can't you vote online? Almost every single study of voter participation tells you these elements will increase turnout. Ask yourself why your local and federal governments are not following these simple questions.

The only answer to continued resistance to these changes is to run. To run yourself. Governments in some parts of the world know that the financial barriers to candidacy are often so high that they can essentially neglect their constituents. Indeed, there's a cycle to voter suppression, one made worse by the corruption of elections through the politics of money. Certain populations are said not to vote, so candidates from those backgrounds and areas can't run because they do not get the money to run. Even when they do get the money to run, their opponents know just which demographics to push down on, whom to scrub from voting rolls. The nakedness of this control mechanism can vandalize any kind of optimism.

Yet each election is a chance to rebuild a politics of optimism. Each candidate is a chance to defeat the cynical politics of voter suppression. So if your vote is being ignored, run. One of the extraordinary aftereffects of the Me Too movement has been a huge surge in female candidates. If government cannot be trusted to protect the rights of women, let alone a woman's right to choose, then the thing to do is to run. Nearly five hundred women ran for congressional primaries alone in 2018 in the United States, which led to the most diverse Congress ever elected, one that looks a lot more like the nation it represents. In a world knitted by social media and crowdsourced funding, smaller candidates have greater weapons than ever in elections. It is possible to run for office without taking major donations or beginning with enormous ad buys.

A cynic might say here that even if someone enters elected office with the noblest of intentions, the politics of power and money will eventually corrupt them. In a world in which most elected officials make terrible compromises, that may be so. Here's why we need a revolution of how we approach civic life, though, and who gets to be involved. Imagine if in coming elections, candidates win who are not corrupted, who were themselves once voters so outraged they ran for office; imagine if a great many of them refused the kinds of strings-attached donations that have led us to the point we are in now, where elected officials say one thing and vote another way on key legislation. What if so many people like this get elected that it's impossible to buy them all—also because they refuse. What would be possible then?

The ubiquity of money in politics today, especially in America, means that one of the most powerful statements a candidate can make is, *I won't take the money.* Voters can signal their desire for this. Peer pressure can, in fact, drive it. Voters can also protest for it. Have you ever watched an election in which one candidate changes a position under duress so that their opponent holding it loses that advantage? With the right amount of protesting and public service ads and a strategic use of social media, voters can make it known that refusing dark money in elections is a must.

These types of changes are necessary to lend power back to the voter. A voter is a mighty thing; a single voter has decided elections. A single voter has led to sweeping social change. A single vote, in, say, a justice system ruling, has led to the overturning of some of the worst and most discriminating practices in many of our societies. A common judicial ruling tally is 5–4. That vote was made possible by your vote. A candidate who talks only of himself gives fair warning that he does not understand this fundamental truth. Change is always driven by and stems from people. The elected official—the person later seen as heroic—often has done something quite simple, decent, and just. People bring to politics an understanding of what they need and how they live. This should not be so hard. Yet society has shown that preserving this relationship requires constant vigilance and questioning. A vote is the most important way to ask, Are you hearing us?

Women

There are no progressive social movements of note without women—be it the abolition of slavery, the stump for the right to vote, or the devastating and ongoing quest to find those who have been disappeared under dictatorships or narco-states, the United States included. Women are the hub around which these and many other movements turn. Primarily because women have had to function as second-class citizens everywhere they have lived. From the moment they become politically conscious, women must learn how and when to fight. They observe the gap between what is thought and what is said, and between what is spoken and what gets done. A woman has to watch these differentials because her safety depends upon it. In the home and on the street and at work. Even a rich white woman, in possession of all the levers of power that attend her, becomes less than the moment she enters a room of men.

And so women are schooled in resistance from a very young age. They are told as children that certain things are unfair, and as children the spokes of injustice stick in their mouths. Your brother can play outside; your brother is allowed to get dirty; your brother will inherit the land;

W

your brother's sexual desires are forgiven; your brother can fight with his hands; your brother can wear pants. If men think girls do not silently slot these unfairnesses into a tally within their heads, we are mistaken. For a long time, men have acted as if women are made by the behavior these subtractions allow: gentleness, kindness, passivity. In fact, women are made by how they deal with the rage this inspires. They are made by the doubleness it creates. To think otherwise is a fantasy.

Among the mistakes men with power have made—other than the primary one of abusing their power—has been an assumption of female apathy. That, in essence, male power would extend forever since women weren't speaking up, or that those who were rarely were heard. Many women learn early not to voice their concerns unselectively: this is imparted to them around the time that all the above lessons are taught to them. And so women may not have been directing resistance upward all the time, but they have always spoken sideways to one another. Whispering. Sharing stories. This invisible network is at once very old and vast. The election of a naked abuser—someone who revels in and brags about his ability to abuse—has activated the network at the highest level in America, and now we're seeing what happens when an invisible grid of support no longer has to be so invisible.

Here's one of the reasons Western societies have felt

so chaotic in recent years. Women's rage is out in the open. In many fields it's no longer bottled, contained, subverted, or distilled into some other behavior. It's in the air. It's on the pages of newspapers; it's in films and culture. It's acted upon. In America, the fastest-rising category of gun ownership is among black women, largely due to the fear of white supremacist violence. Men, since the beginning of time, have had the power to tamp down women's rage, to label and ostracize it. To belittle it. Even to mock it as hysteria. Now they cannot do this so easily, because so many women are expressing it from positions of power that it cannot be ignored. It has consequences.

This cultural whiplash in Western society has been shocking and confusing. It has been liberating. It is ongoing—and its work is just beginning to be accomplished. The revelations of sexual abuse and assault, for instance, are so widespread that most societies need to come to grips with the fact that rape is an epidemic. That it has been one of the primary ways that power has been enforced between men and women. Men who have not been sexually assaulted themselves cannot even begin to imagine the secret power this threat enforces. Talking about it, however, making it visible, has begun to reduce the coercive power of rape culture only for a select few. For all the ways life has been made safer in certain industries, in other fields it's still not safe for women to come forward. Women who are undocumented, for instance, and women who are poor; women who do not have access to the media. Women who do not have public personas. Women who don't have the time to agitate in public squares. Women who are beaten secretly or in public arenas where that does not yet constitute a break from the norm.

If the ongoing reckoning does not expand to include all women, it will simply reiterate the levers of power that fall heavily on female bodies everywhere—those of race, class, and ethnicity. The lottery of where in the world one is born. The work of doing this extension should not just fall to women. Nor should it be perceived as proceeding only from naming and shaming. In fact, there are possibilities in this moment that do not stem from destruction. After all, the network women created and used for so long to navigate what could not be said publicly has always had fellow travelers. It has in the best of moments included and protected children, the weak, and anyone else whose neck has been under the boot of a power and who still does not relent. It's why women were essential to the Underground Railroad, to the creation of social networks, to the spread of capitalism. Women as homemakers were essential to the creation of consumer markets.

The possibilities of this moment, if its travelers take the ethical dilemma of inclusiveness on board, are endless. Men and women have suffered together (though not equally) under the power of men for a long time, and there is strength in acknowledging that solidarity. Many men raised to be masculine in ways that equated abuses of power with masculinity—be it as sons, workers, or citizens—feel relief at recent changes. They are cheering them. This intersection of relief and possibility will become harder yet to see if the reckoning begins to see justice entirely in binary terms: women taking power from men, or women replacing or usurping men, or men resisting both of these moments. Some men clearly see the reckoning in this way. So, too, have some women. And sometimes, of course, they will be right, and sometimes that replacement in fact will be just. A woman should not need to be the most overqualified candidate in the history of elections to challenge a barely literate man in a presidential race, for example. Still, as with financial inequality, the current imbalance of power impoverishes both men and women. There are huge communities around the world in which the shared experience of dealing with this imbalance of power between men and women is deep and generational, complex. It has shaped a great many people; taking away or reducing the imbalance cannot change the shape we've been molded to so rapidly.

Our challenge, in all our societies, is to figure out ways to create an expanded social space in which the complexity of change we are facing can be absorbed, narrated, and paid tribute. Women and men from previous movements who believe in gender-based equality need to be part of the discussion in order to avoid this. In the meantime, culturally, we must not forget the work of the past. Some of it can be done in finally acknowledging what has always been there. For instance, why aren't there equal numbers of monuments to women in public spaces and on banknotes? Even Jane Austen is on a note in the U.K. Is there a reason Edith Wharton isn't on one in America? Or Zora Neale Hurston? Imagine what that would do for kids growing up spending a Wharton, not just a Lincoln—or even later in the future, a Morrison (let alone a Tubman—thwarted, for now, by the current U.S. government). What if teachers were taught that it was the norm to listen to girls and boys equally? What kind of learning environment would that create? What kind of questions would unfold in a classroom in which half the participants weren't being pressed down? What knowledge have we denied ourselves? Would we as nations resort so quickly to killing our way out of disputes if women were equally represented in the legislative bodies? We don't know the answers to these questions because they have never been tested. Treating women with equal respect and dignity should not just be the goal of this revolution; it's the solution that's been in front of us.

Anonymous

Before their names rise to print like beads of hot metal, anonymous people often tell us what we need to know. They tell us who the cheaters and thieves are in our societies. They explain when our governments are lying. Who is dumping toxic material into groundwater. Who thinks citizens are looking the other way. Where the bodies are buried. Who hid the murder weapon. In a climate of constant rolling attacks on the power of the press and law enforcement, it's useful to remember: anonymous but verified sources create the smelting fires of investigative journalism and of serious investigations, without which our societies are essentially at the whim of governments and corporations and the powerful.

It sounds absurd to have to state it plainly, but without someone or many people watching them, agitating for truth—all these institutions will lie. Governments, corporations, the powerful. They will fabricate gas mileage numbers or studies about the lethality of their products. They will tell us the war is going well; they will claim the president had no connection to the break-in. They will make a mockery of the tax code, or bury their enemies, or collaborate with competitors. It's not just that power corrupts: power, when it reaches the stage of imbalance we currently see, encourages impunity. To grab and take in plain sight.

This is a very dangerous stage of tyranny. It means essentially that norms and decency no longer matter, that even a correct accusation cannot stop the activity from continuing. All that is left then—when public apathy has been leveraged—is the law. You will witness a startling number of lawsuits, civil action suits, and legal maneuvers to stop outright thievery in America at this moment. For a long time, the United States has bragged to the world that it was an experiment in democracy. At this stage, however, the democratic experiment seems to have morphed into a different kind of enterprise: a new form of tyranny—a soft tyranny of opt-in subscribers.

Tyrannical power does not always arrive in the form of a mustachioed strongman. It sometimes takes the shape of an intersection of interests: of political and corporate power overlapping in a way that defrauds common citizens of their rights, of fair government. The fig leaf in these moments is elections—the powers that be can claim there was an election and people voted. This may be true, but when fewer and fewer people vote, and when elections themselves are compromised by repressive tactics, and then the elected officials so often vote against the interests of their constituents, democracy has ceased to function.

This form of democracy in ritual only has been enabled by the defunding of public education and the destruction of the information environment. If citizens do not have a sense of context, one developed through education and thought, then propaganda and outright hate-mongering can be incredibly powerful. It is far easier to blame a person or a type of person for the loss of one's job or standing in society than a complex systemic failure. In the battle between left and right the world over, the right has banked heavily on hatred and on leveraging this ignorance. On leveraging nationalism.

To stoke these feelings, governments will lie constantly and often. A government by one definition is an entity answerable to its citizens. A more cynical and current definition is a government is a body that lies to its citizens. This might be funny were it not so true in many of our states. In the age of the internet, the speed of information and communication moves so fast that a government has often moved on to a new lie by the time an old one has been revealed to be false. The speed of this game of leapfrog leads the press to make two mistakes: First, to believe that their job is to catch people lying. This is a side effect of living under tyrannies. Second, to make the lies the story.

X

Lies are no more unique to a tyrannical government than breathing is to a human being. Lying is simply a way to create space to keep doing what they are doing. The challenge of the press and of investigative law enforcement in such a scenario often has little to do with the main source of the lie—the CEO or, say, the president. It often requires getting to the heart of a narrative of what happened. Or what is happening. What actions are being covered up and who they benefit. If a head of state was bribed, the question isn't why but how. Who paid, who transferred the money, into what bank account, and under what pretense? Which bankers participated in the action, and did they know what they were doing?

Getting answers to such questions requires anonymous sources. A press that agitates. Someone inside an operation who is disturbed by the actions but cannot run the risk of exposing themselves. In some instances, they want to avoid this limelight for personal reasons; in others, they know they may wind up dead, or beaten, or with their lives in ruin. Power creates and implies its own kinds of threats. It makes examples of those who cross it. Most criminal enterprises punish traitors grotesquely. They are decapitated, defenestrated, hanged in public. They are shamed in embarrassing ways. This has to happen only a few times for people to get the message: We can make your life a living hell. In a state still run under law and order, the discomfort can be dealt out in milder but still excruciating ways. Recently, the U.S. president caused the pension of a civil servant to be taken. In the course of the bullying campaign, the civil servant and his family also received death threats. They were so afraid, they employed extra protection.

You can spot tyranny by how hard it tries to undermine any kind of watchdog group, the press, institutional law enforcement. Tyrants threaten or ban reporters, accidentally shoot them in war zones, prosecute leakers, and throw journalists in jail when they will not reveal sources. They expose anonymous sources in investigations; they even expose spies whose message they do not like. They label them treasonous, when in fact it is the actions of tyranny that make up that definition.

The harder powers that be make it to report upon what they are doing, the more essential anonymous sources become. Anonymous sources make it impossible for tyrannical powers to entirely shape the media around their narratives. When anonymous sources come forward, the press is empowered to do far more than react to what a government or corporation says: it can ask questions about what they are doing.

To find, develop, hear, and ultimately vet anonymous sources costs money, though. It takes a great deal of time. This is not day-to-day-reaction reporting. It means forging a relationship, listening for hours and days at a time. It can mean getting calls in the middle of the night and disrupting one's own life to prove responsiveness, to answer the call when at last the source is ready to speak. The intersection of corporate and political power that gave birth to a free internet has been devastating to news organizations. Somehow, newspapers are meant to provide the same kind of coverage of local and world events and speak truth to power without any of their former revenue source—advertising.

It's not working. Bit by bit, investigative journalism—the most expensive but also most crucial part of the news—is becoming too costly to provide. The powers that be are already celebrating. Imagine what the powers that be can do without a watchful press. They won't even have to lie, as no one will actually know what to ask them. Most tyrannies work inward from this point, purging law enforcement of anyone who attempts to investigate them. An overwhelmed press doesn't know where to look—to the flamboyant larceny happening in public? The outright aggression against citizens? The sidelining of law enforcement who can call the tyranny to account? This flooding of the zone is done on purpose, and there's only one person who can make it stop.

You There is no clanging ambulance on the way. No sled pulled through the avalanche. No helicopter rescue. No phone call in the night to say *Now is the time.* We have watched and we have watched and we have watched a rising tyranny take hold in so many parts of this globe. We stood by as organizations that secured the eight-hour workday and the right not to eat rotten meat were blithely destroyed. As presidents swept the chips into their pile before our eyes. We bargained away our health care, our schools. Our digits said thumbs-up to no privacy. All the terrible things were over there. Well, now it's night's close, and we the people have very little. In some places we can speak; in others not. In some places we can vote; in others not. In some places our bodies are illegal; in others not. But in too many places all of us are barely getting by while a criminal amount of wealth and power is held by a very few.

In far too many places we feel far too close to a roll-back of modernity.

You are the only way out. Only you can do something. They might get their act together, but chances are they won't. Who gives up power? Usually it's someone who *has to* forfeit their power. He might do it for you, but he cannot be counted on; she, perhaps. Women in fact do far too much; they know this—they have learned one of the key things to know is how to say no. So as you read this, the network of responsibility that you feel held by, supported in, it has become threadbare. Now it's your turn to weave a little decency back into it. You don't have to stand before a house of Parliament and read a poem, or attend a vigil at a politician's office, or shout questions in a public hearing, or write letters to the heads of global companies. You can start with just one thing, one act of optimism. One a week, one a day. Maybe just a small gesture. Maybe opening a door for someone else.

Life is, in fact, a blizzard of these gestures. People are kinder in the real world, too, than they are online. So live, if you can, a little more there. Throw your first gesture at making the real world a little better, a little kinder, a richer, less-toxic environment. It's like drinking tap water rather than bottled water once a day. What if more made the same choice? Would we have islands of trash in our oceans the size of small countries? That's an accumulation of terrible gestures. A disposable culture says, It's your problem; here, you take care of it. But that's not a fair way to live. To embrace a world of trash is to say that some of us are, essentially, trash. All of us know what sort of imbalances this blizzard of gestures has brought today.

A world where twenty-six people own more than half the world.

It can be undone by you, though. Begin with small gestures; that's how hope starts. It's a match in the dark, not a bonfire. Strike it. Give someone a coin; listen to a friend longer than you want to. Walk an extra block home to mail a postcard from your local post office rather than send an email. Bike to a farmer's market to buy your produce from a farmer. Read the newspaper and write back to your columnist, on a piece of paper. Write a letter of thanks to your child's teacher. Encourage people to save up some time to take a few hours off work to vote, to vote early. Watch one less TV show and dedicate one-third of that time to attending political rallies, marching for things you want to happen. Spend a weekend walking door-to-door to talk to people you want to come with you. Introduce yourself to them. Listen to them tell you what they care about—and why. March with women.

One of the things scientists now know is that it's not great being you, unless you relate to others. *I* is in fact one of the loneliest letters: anonymous whistle-blowers know this. Yet to be an I, to be a me, is presented and sold to us like the best thing to be. How much better it is to be more than one, especially when that addition is made through generosity. To have your coffee mysteriously paid for when you're broke. To be given an umbrella by another. To have a hand extended when you're climbing into a bus. To feel the arms of another standing next to you in a house of worship, at a concert, at a funeral. To know you are not alone.

Yes, someone has just read these sentences thinking, I hate other people. Good for you. But before we write you off, have you tried talking to a person in a nursing home? What about a child who needs tutoring? The person sitting alone at a baseball game? Even the misanthropic among us know that it feels better to be part of some kind of group than to be alone by the fire of our television. This is the feeble warmth we have been sold and bought into—the idea that we can entertain ourselves away from the terrible knowledge that our time is brief and that the world, as it stands now, we cannot and we should not abide.

You should listen to the part of you that cries out with this knowledge. Cries out in your sleep. Sees in the eyes of your own child another. Our world in fact depends upon this response. It is how a politics of optimism develops—not one small political drill after another, one devastating tweet or two. But one act at a time. One act of resistance in the form of love. Loving radically and freely. Loving without restriction. Loving without questions as to whether a person is worthy. Loving because it's how to be, it feels good, and it's the best way one can say to the takers and grifters, You can take a lot, but you may not take my dignity or my decency.

Think of how the world would work if we took all the rage wasted online and directed that energy back to one another in positive ways. Back into our own lives— rather than at the living monuments of power. How many gestures, small or otherwise, would be possible then? What tiny part of momentum would tip toward justice? A gesture of kindness is a strange thing: In some cases it makes a moment pass, perhaps more easily. In others it leaves behind a trace that almost guides you toward a norm of kindness. In this way small gestures, even if they are not your own, accumulate. They create pathways of togetherness, or at least a ghost map that says, We are not alone in this life, and we need to, we must, work together to make it easier on one another. It's the obvious thing to do.

A tyrant or a tyrannically tipped world takes energy to maintain. Messages have to be sent, opposition intimidated, beaten, agitated against, or even killed. It is not the natural order, even if you subscribe to the idea that we're only a mere few thousand years as a species from a much more fearful and violent daily reality. Historically this is true, but among the powers of our civilizations are the protections and freedoms, the safety enlarged togetherness has brought. Also the pleasure. The more of us who live together in this *we*, the more of the world we can experience in what we eat, what we listen to, what threads we wear, and what rituals we can make our own, or at least observe.

You can assert the value of this all by yourself. You do not need a battalion behind you; it already exists. We are all there with you, silently asserting that this cannot abide. Saying it one gesture at a time. One protest at a time. One election at a time. One decision at a time, as much as we can, and sometimes even more. No one else can make you start extending—you have that power. It is, in fact, one of your last. If you are reading this, that means you still have it. Use it. Ask the questions. Hold the door open for the one behind you. Strike the match.

Zygote

We are born into this world slippery and ignorant, sea creatures with crusted eyes. Salt-slick and blood-flecked. Unspeaking, barely seeing, and terrified. Agitating for love. We are delivered from the sea of our wombs into a world of solids, sounds, other people. We fasten hard to one person—our mother, if she is there—then begin the long road to decreaturing ourselves. Learning how to use our limbs, our voice boxes, our own particular languages, separating ourselves from others. We discover how to share, speak, love, and then operate in a world defined by nations, norms, and what we're entitled to as citizens. We learn, hopefully, how to articulate when that is not enough, as is almost always the case. We say it with our tongues, pay for it with our bodies.

It is remarkable how all this is contained in the complexity of a zygote, that fertilized cell, the result of two becoming one. Every single capacity of my body sitting here, saying this to you, calls from that remarkable thing when an object starts becoming a human being. If only we could think of ourselves as zygotes still, bodies teeming with a trillion possibilities, selves, hundreds of thousands of maps where destination and journey are contained on the same plane. We learn too soon that fate and character are entwined, that some people are just different. That on this planet falling through the dark, some struck out on the lottery of life; surely when that idea of living is accepted, whole cities of possibility within the zygote that is you brown out, like a power grid sabotaged in some act of midnight vandalism.

One of the points of this book has been to navigate around the rhetorical acts of sabotage, to grab the pump levers of language and turn the lights back on. You can call it spirit or you can call it a soul, but deep inside us there is something bigger than ourselves, and the way that capacity has become an action and then part of a society has and always will be language. We live by breathing, we exist by doing, we do both together by communicating— taking breath and turning it into a concept others can understand, can take some measure of. All across the globe we're watching a frontal assault on this device. It's being hacked to pieces in plain sight. Words emptied of meaning, turned into weapons, objects; the etymology decoupled, decontextualized. It's not a linguistic experiment. It's an instinctual act of violence. Words are what connect us: a shared belief that the world is there and can be described and our tongues, languages, mouths make that possible. The number one goal of tyrants is to insert themselves into the space between and assert that only they can explain, define, determine. They do not want us speaking, writing, and talking to one another. They want us looking to them. Think hard where the attention in your media goes; how much of it goes in one direction?

We are better than this, the zygote says, because there's an infinite array of possibilities in the zygote. There is disease and disruption, yes, but also a breathtaking capacity for intelligence; for giving, which is intelligence in action; and for optimism, which is giving conceptualized into potential action. We know this because when a baby is born of the right circumstances, the feeling in that room or hospital, in the birth or adoptive parents' arms when they hold the baby, is love. Possibility made flesh; love made living; nostalgia instantly turned inside out into hope. As we arrow through our days, the best parts of that experience can be removed from us by aerodynamics. It is almost as hard to carry hope as it is to carry pain. Experience so often tells us to let hope go. It is difficult to ferry love through a world that takes such pleasure in the vicious denial of it to people considered less than, to an environment those same governments treat as less than a resource—as loot.

We are better than this. Our zygote tells us so. The point of this book is to reclaim that potential by opening up the words that have been buried in plain sight. We cannot have fairness becoming part of a time capsule of our governments. Nor decency. Those concepts are not just ideas; they make everyday life possible. If they are stripped from public life, we are in very bad shape indeed. We cannot be a society if we worship the self and the all-empowered I as much as we do today. We will never be able to communicate if all our voices are the most important, the most essential, the most wounded, the most traumatized, the most entitled, the most articulate, the most powerful. The funniest. Has it not occurred to you that in acting this way, we are rehearsing the behavior and entitlement of an all-powerful leader? That by trying on these types of presumptions, we are allowing ourselves to be inched toward a sense of déjà vu when that person arrives on the public stage? That we are preparing to identify with that person? This is the twenty-first-century way into fascism.

We are better than this apathy in the face of environmental genocide, this apathy in a time of killing. We will not undo this damage by usurping power. We need to revolutionize our societies, from the zygote up, and reclaim the mysteries and multiplicity in that fertilized cell with language that does the same. Language that enlarges rather than diminishes. We need to begin articulating who we are with this language and what we want, building newer monuments than the ones that are trying to erect themselves before us. We are better than police states. We are better than reactions; we can agitate for better questions. We are better than our rage, our sabotage, our dumbing down, and our denigrating our very teachers. If we are going to live in civil societies, if we are going to vote, we need to expand what we are voting for, we need more women involved, and we need all of ourselves and all of our language to do that, not this mutilated instrument we see in the public eye that so many of our leaders flog before us, surveilling our reactions.

It is not enough to make fun of them. We are better than our cynicism. Nor does it suffice to simply comment on social media. We have to work, in small groups, person to person, locally, to rebuild our sense of values from the ground up. At town hall meetings, meals, religious services, lectures, literary events, work, school, cafés, in the street, in conversations, in local elections, in letters to one another.

Above us, in the ozone of national politics, in so many of our nations, leaders are turning language and, by extension, all the possibilities of the zygote into a scrap heap. They don't even plan to use the slag. The more it's degraded, the less they need to live and operate by human values. The inequality of our world is not sustainable, nor is it human. We are going to change this, one day and one moment at a time, on our own and with each other. We can begin by saying this does not suffice; we will no longer abide. We all need language to be as specific as possible. To be at least twenty-six words strong. Let's start with these.

AFTERWORD by Valeria Luiselli

Thought may be a deeply personal, internal, at times solitary process, but it is also the most collective of activities. It is collective because it is done with words, and those words belong not just to the person who uses them, but to an entire linguistic community. Or perhaps words don't belong to a community—nobody can own language—as much as they are the very threads that bind us to one another: they give us foundational myths; they give us stories; they produce philosophy, friendship, criticism, politics, humor; they are the midwives of social revolutions and change.

Words may bind us, but they can also become weapons against us, and particularly against the less powerful and more vulnerable members of a society. In the hands of the powerful—be it the political or economic elite, or the racial or military supremacy—words can become a particularly potent, cruel weapon. If the objective of power is to remain stable or to further consolidate, that is, to protect the status quo or transform into tyranny, everyday language will be used to perpetuate imbalances. A racial elite, for example, will protect the status quo, calling everyone who is not like them a "minority"—a term itself apparently harmless, and merely numerical in its primary connotation, but one that carries another set of associations that both reflect and preserve imbalance of power and political capital. Then there is the word *illegal*, which, when used to refer to a sector of a population that does not have passports or visas, becomes an ideological weapon against an already disenfranchised group of people. It converts individuals into criminals, and justifies political and institutional violence against them: detention, incarceration, denial of medical attention, denial of due process. The word *illegal* is still, today, used as common currency, despite the fact that it is dehumanizing, despite its exercising a brutal psychological violence on an individual's mind; despite the fact of it being completely nonsensical: What is an *illegal person*?

We cannot assume that words are just there for us to use—selfishly, irresponsibly, like an inexhaustible resource. Thoughtless use of words, especially those that contain complex meanings and various connotations, may serve to perpetrate and perpetuate violence. It is our responsibility, therefore, as members of a linguistic community, to engage in the daily task of thinking about and rethinking the kind of violence that words can exert, and that can easily go by, unnoticed. We are all responsible for keeping words, and the complex tapestry we are endlessly creating and undoing with them across decades and centuries, safe from the possibility of being transformed into instruments of violence. The only way to do that is to think, constantly and with a sense of collectivity, about the words that circulate among us. And it really is crucial that everyone remain actively involved in the ongoing process of revising and renewing the language we use, because that is the only way to ensure that words will not be hijacked by those in power, the only way that our minds will not be dominated by them, be that power a tyrannical political leader, political parties owned by lobbyists, or the companies that surveil us through the internet.

The Spanish philosopher Maria Zambrano, exiled during Francisco Franco's dictatorship, devoted much of her writing to thinking about what happens to words and to thought in times of totalitarian regimes. She writes about the loss of a sense of community in the suffocating atmosphere of those regimes: "Under such conditions, when we want to relate to our fellow men and women, who find themselves in a similar situation, it is simply impossible to live with others, and consequently, to live." Zambrano, like Hannah Arendt or Primo Levi, as well as many of the other thinkers who had to flee into exile in the midst of persecution, also wrote about the vital role that thought plays in undoing the harm that totalitarianism causes both to an individual's interiority and to his or her capacity to relate to others, to coexist with others. "One of the essential functions of thought," she writes, "is to make the atmosphere breathable, to free human beings from asphyxia, which is caused by a lack of inner space, when conscience becomes filled with shadows, with uncertainty; when the shadows of others and our own shadow have made our inner space, the primary space in which we move and breathe, excessively opaque." The triad of thought/interiority/community is a revindication of what totalitarianism seeks to take away from people. Individuals living under totalitarianism feel more distanced from each other: mistrustful, confused, isolated. The means by which power achieves this is by controlling the discourse—making concepts opaque, instilling fear and uncertainty, filling us with noise. Survival depends on our capacity to think clearly and freely. And, of course, collectively.

John Freeman has been actively seeking and facilitating collective thinking for several years now, both as a writer and as an editor. All his projects feel like an invitation to enter into a polyphonic, multi-voiced conversation with other minds. *Dictionary of the Undoing* is no different. It is a book that makes you think, then rethink. It invites you to engage with it, to refute it, to contribute to it. At the same time, it invites you to understand thought as the collective process that it is and reminds you that thought, when it turns around to look at itself and the words with which it is made possible, becomes charged with the particular energy of collectivity. Or, perhaps, with hope, which Freeman defines as "less an emotion than a field, a magnetism." He writes: "Put bodies near each other and hope happens."

Dictionary of the Undoing, as its author states, is an effort to build a "lexicon of engagement." It is not a dictionary, though its structure follows an alphabetical order. It isn't a book of definitions, despite its preoccupation with sense and meaning. More than anything, it is a book that works in the same way we make constellations. A handful of luminous presences in the dark and unfathomable space of our minds are placed in relation, one to the other. From there emerges a shape, a figure that both contains and suggests meanings. Concepts that seem distant from one another, if thought about relationally, will yield meaning. Take, for example, the word *justice*, the word *rage*, and the word *women*. What shapes emerge from combining those words? What questions do they elicit? Or take the words *artificial intelligence, police, race,* and *environment*: a dystopic constellation is likely to appear. Then introduce the words *hope* and *question*, and perhaps something else emerges.

Dictionary of the Undoing is one thinker's firmament, full of possible constellations. It is a snapshot of a mind in a specific moment of history, looking inward to find clusters of meaning that might shine some light on the darkness outside. It undertakes the urgent task of finding clarity internally in order to then be able to engage collectively, all in the hope that the atmosphere around us may once more become breathable. It undertakes the urgent task of thought. And it invites us to do the same.

Palermo, 2019

ACKNOWLEDGMENTS This book began as an attempt to feel less alone in a period that seems designed to isolate us. Some friends were crucial to it. Aleksandar Hemon and Rebecca Solnit in particular told me to write it. I'm deeply grateful to both for the challenge. I'm also indebted to Sarah Burnes and Elena Marcu for reading along as I wrote it, possibly the kindest (and most insane) thing to do for a writer. Sean McDonald judiciously and patiently turned it into a book, Rodrigo Corral and Richard Oriolo made it look like one, and James Gurbutt and Ida Hamidovic gave early flags of faith when they were most needed. Thank you too to Kerri Arsenault for putting it through the oven of her intelligence. Thanks to Rebecca Gardner for helping it find friends, to Valeria Luiselli for lending her mind to its ideas, to Stella Soffía Jóhannesdóttir, Aminatta Forna, and Deborah Landau for giving me space to see if it made sense before an audience. Danny Vazquez and Stephen Weil, thank you for helping me reach its finish line. Sections of this text appeared in *Corriere della Serra*, *Illustrada in Foelho de São Paolo*, *Korean Literature Today*, and *Orion*. I'm especially thankful to Sumanth Prabhaker for his edits to the chapter on environment. Finally, Nicole Aragi heard parts of this aloud on mornings I'm sure she would rather have started the day with Mal Waldron. For that and so much else, thank you.